API Archi

The Big Picture for Building APIs

by Matthias Biehl

API University Series
www.api-university.com

API-University Press

Copyright © 2015 by Matthias Biehl

All rights reserved, including the right to reproduce
this book or portions thereof in any form whatsoever.

ISBN-13: 978-1508676645
ISBN-10: 150867664X

3

4

Synopsis

Looking for the big picture of building APIs? This book is for you!

Building APIs that consumers love should certainly be the goal of any API initiative. However, it is easier said than done. It requires getting the architecture for your APIs right. This book equips you with both foundations and best practices for API architecture. This book presents best practices for putting an infrastructure in place that enables efficient development of APIs.

This book is for you if you want to understand the big picture of API design and development, you want to define an API architecture, establish a platform for APIs or simply want to build APIs your consumers love.

This book is NOT for you, if you are looking for a step-by step guide for building APIs, focusing on every detail of the correct application of REST principles. In this case I recommend the book API Design of the API-University Series.

What is API architecture? Architecture spans the bigger picture of APIs and can be seen from several perspectives:

API architecture may refer to the architecture of the complete solution consisting not only of the API itself, but also of an API client such as a mobile app and several other components. API solution architecture explains the components and their relations within the software solution.

API architecture may refer to the technical architecture of the API platform. When building, running and exposing not only one, but several APIs, it becomes clear that certain building blocks of the API, runtime functionality and management functionality for the API need to be used over and over again. An API platform provides an infrastructure for developing, running and managing APIs.

API architecture may refer to the architecture of the API portfolio. The API portfolio contains all APIs of the enterprise and needs to be managed like a product. API portfolio architecture analyzes the functionality of the API and organizes, manages and reuses the APIs.

API architecture may refer to the design decisions for a particular API proxy. To document the design decisions, API description languages are used. We explain the use of API description languages (RAML and Swagger) on many examples.

This book covers all of the above perspectives on API architecture. However, to become useful, the architecture needs to be put into practice. This is why this book covers an API methodology for design and development. An API methodology provides practical guidelines for putting API architecture into practice. It explains how to develop an API architecture into an API that consumers love.

A lot of the information on APIs is available on the web. Most of it is published by vendors of API products. I am always a bit suspicious of technical information pushed by product vendors. This book is different. In this book, a product-independent view on API architecture is presented.

The API-University Series is a modular series of books on API-related topics. Each book focuses on a particular API topic, so you can select the topics within APIs, which are relevant for you.

Keywords: API, API Management, API Architecture, Integration, API Description Languages, RAML, Swagger

Table of Contents

Introduction 15
   What is an API? 15
   Why APIs? 16
   How are APIs used? 18
   How to build APIs? 18
   What is API Architecture? 20
   How to put API Architecture into Practice? 21
   Why is API Architecture Important? 22

API Solution Architecture 25
   Types of API Solutions 26
     Mobile Solutions 26
     Cloud Solutions 27
     Web Solutions 27
     Integration Solutions 28
     Multi-Channel Solutions 29
     Smart TV Solutions 29
     Internet of Things 30
   Stakeholders in API Solutions 31
     API Providers 31
     API Consumers 33
     End Users 33
   API-related Design Decisions 34
     What do all types of API solutions have in common? ... 34
     Functionality in the Client or in the API? 35
     Use an existing API or build a new API? 35
     How to choose a third party API? 36

API Platform Architecture 39
   Overview 40

8

API Development Platform 41
   Library of API Building Blocks............................... 42
   Language for Implementing APIs 43
   Language for Designing APIs 44
API Runtime Platform 45
API Engagement Platform 46
API Platform Configurations and Interactions 48
   Environments.. 48
   API Platform Deployment Models............................ 49
   Interactions between the Platforms 49
Surrounding Systems 51
   Load Balancers and Firewalls............................... 53
   Identity and Access Management Infrastructure 53
   Existing Functionality in Backends 54
   New Functionality 55
   Enterprise Service Buses and SOA Platforms.............. 55

API Portfolio Architecture 59
Requirements 59
   Consistency 59
   Reuse 60
   Customization 61
   Discoverability... 61
   Longevity 62
Governance.. 62
Consistency 63
   Consistency Checks in Practice 64
Reuse 65
   Reuse of API Features 65
   Reuse of Complete APIs 66
   Reusing own APIs 66
   Reusing Third-Party APIs 67
Customization.. 68
   Approach 70
   Summary 71

Discoverability 71
   Manual Discovery 72
   Automated Discovery... 72
Change Management and Versioning........................ 74
   The Evolution Challenge... 74
   Why does the Evolution Challenge exist at all?...................... 75
   Classifying API Evolution 75
   Dealing with Evolution in APIs 78
   Anticipating and Avoiding Evolution.............................. 79
   Prevent Feature Creep 80

API Proxy Architecture 83
Requirements for APIs 83
   Responsibilities of APIs 84
   Desirable Properties of APIs...................................... 85
Architectural Patterns 88
   Client Server Patterns... 88
   Facade Pattern 90
   Proxy Pattern 91
Architectural Styles... 91
   REST Style 92
   HATEOAS Style.. 96
   RPC Style 97
   SOAP Style.. 99
   Architectural Trade-offs 99

API Description Languages 105
What are API Description Languages?.................. 106
   API Description Language vs. API Development Language 107
Usage 108
   Communication and Documentation...................... 108
   Design Repository 110
   Contract Negotiation 111
   API Implementation 112
   Client Implementation 113
   Discovery 113

Simulation 114

Language Features 114

Swagger 117

Introduction 117

Example 118

Root Element 120

Resources 122

Parameters 126

Reusable Elements 128

Security 129

RAML 133

Introduction 133

Example 134

Root Element 136

Resources 137

Schema 138

Parameters 139

Reusable Elements 143

Security 145

Summary 147

API Methodology 151

Foundations 151

Consumer-oriented Design Approach 152

Contract First Design Approach 154

Agile Design Approach 154

Simulation-based Design 155

Requirements for an API Methodology 156

Methodology 158

Overview 158

Phase 1: Domain Analysis 159

Phase 2: Architectural Design 162

Phase 3: Prototyping 164

Phase 4: Implementation for Production 167

Phase 5: Publish 168

11

Maintenance 171

Discussion 172
   Hand-over Points 172
   Pre-Work vs. Actual Work...................................... 173

Summary 174

Conclusion 177

Backmatter 181

Feedback 181

About the Author 181

Other Products by the Author.............................. 182
   OAuth 2.0: API Security Book................................ 182
   API Design Book.. 183
   OAuth 2.0 Online Course...................................... 184

References 187

Image Sources 190

Introduction

What is an API?

Software is typically used by people like you and me via a user interface. Increasingly, however, software is not only used by people, but also by other software applications. This requires another type of interface, an Application Programming Interface, in short API.

APIs offer a simple way for connecting to, integrating with and extending a software system. More precisely, APIs are used for building distributed software systems, whose components are loosely coupled. The APIs studied here are web-APIs, which are realized as web services and deliver data resources via a web technology stack. Typical applications using APIs are mobile apps, cloud apps, web applications or smart devices.

The charm of APIs is that they are simple, clean, clear and approachable. They provide a reusable interface that different applications can connect to easily. However, APIs do not offer a user interface, they are usually not visible on the surface and typically no end user will directly interact with them. Instead, APIs operate under the hood and are only directly called by other applications. APIs are used for machine to machine communication and for the integration of two or more software systems.

The only people interacting with APIs directly are the developers creating applications or solutions with the APIs. This is why APIs need to be built with the developers in mind, who will integrate the APIs into new applications. This insight explains, why a new perspective is required for building APIs.

Why APIs?

An API offers a simple way for connecting to, integrating with and extending software systems. Now, think about the entities that are run by software. Businesses, markets and banks are run by software. Industrial production processes are controlled by software. Machines, cars and many consumer products contain software. However, these software systems are typically isolated and functionality of one system cannot be accessed from the other system. APIs provide a possibility to connect these separate software entities.

APIs provide the capabilities which are essential for connecting, extending and integrating software. And by connecting software, APIs connect businesses with other businesses, businesses with their products, services with products or products directly with other products.

The infrastructure for enabling this connection is already in place. Each and every person, each employee and each customer has a smart, internet-enabled device, businesses have websites and web-services. Even an increasing number of the products sold by the businesses carry digital sensors and are internet enabled. All these devices are connected to the internet and can - in principle - be connected via APIs.

Just one example for the business to business integration: The business of an enterprise can be expanded by linking the business to partners up and down the value chain. Since businesses are run by IT, the businesses can be better linked by integrating the IT systems of a business up and down the value chain to the IT systems of other businesses, partners, employees and to customers. This can be accomplished if the IT systems of the business partners are linked via services.

An enterprise cannot force its business partners to use its services. But it can make these services so good -- so valuable and simple -- that the business partners will want to use them. If these services are good, they can become a means for retaining existing partners and a means for obtaining new partners.

But what makes a service good? In this context a service is good if

- it is valuable and helps the partners perform their business.

- it fits the exact needs of the partners.

- it is simple to understand.

- it is easy to integrate and monitor for the partners.

- it is secure, reliable and performant.

Generally, APIs are services that deliver several advantageous properties. This is why they are used for both external integration with business partners and for internal integration within the company. Amazon, for example, uses APIs internally, to integrate the IT systems of its departments. If the interfaces and technology are already in place for internal integration, it becomes easier to provide external integration. External integration is used with business partners or external entities. External APIs are also necessary for realizing mobile apps. Interesting mobile apps use company data, data that is delivered to the app via APIs.

Another reason for using APIs is their use as an innovation lab of the enterprise. To fulfill this vision, the API portfolio should enable the enterprise to build innovative apps with little effort and spark creativity. By making company assets easily available through API, new uses of these assets can be found. Since APIs provide a new, simple way for accessing company assets, assets can be used in new ways within the company. Providing external access to company assets, enables third party developers, who are not even on your pay roll, to create innovations for your organization.

How are APIs used?

APIs are not called by end-users directly. Instead, APIs are called by apps, such as mobile apps, web apps or TV apps. The apps are then offered to end users. The complete solution, which uses APIs, typically consists of:

- A client or app that calls the APIs and processes the data provided by the APIs. This client is responsible for the end-user experience.

- A number of APIs that provide the data to the app.

- An API platform that manages the APIs.

How to build APIs?

I will get back to APIs in a moment. For now, let us assume that we were in the car manufacturing business and we would like to build a new car... What would we have to do?

1. We find out, how the consumer would want to use the new car.

2. We design the car, so it fits into the portfolio of different models that our company sells - sports cars, vans and trucks.

3. We choose the architectural style, i.e. if the car uses a diesel engine, hybrid engine or a fully electric engine.

4. We design a blueprint of the car according to the consumer's needs and wants. We simulate components of the car and build a prototype.

5. We select the component suppliers of our car parts.

6. Finally, we configure the assembly line for putting all the car parts together efficiently.

Could work. And what would the corresponding steps be, when building an API?

1. We find out, how the majority of consumers would want to use the new API.

2. We design the API, so it fits into the portfolio of different APIs that our company offers.

3. We choose the architectural style, i.e. if the API applies a REST, RPC or SOAP style.

4. We design a blueprint of the API using an API description language, such as RAML or Swagger. We simulate the API and build a prototype of the API.

5. We select the API platform, which provides the reusable building blocks for the APIs.

6. Finally, we use a generative API methodology to develop APIs efficiently. Of course, the generative techniques are only used as far as possible, at some point some code might still need to be written.

What is API Architecture?

What most API design books focus on is the use of HTTP methods, URI design, HTTP status codes, HTTP headers and the structure of the resources in the HTTP body. However, this is actually the smallest challenge when building APIs. The real challenge is finding an API architecture and defining the methodology.

API architecture is way more than the correct application of REST principles. So what is API architecture? API Architecture spans the bigger picture of APIs and can be seen from several perspectives:

API architecture may refer to the architecture of the complete solution, consisting not only of the API itself, but also of an API client such as a mobile app and several other components. API solution architecture explains the components and their relations within the software solution.

API architecture may refer to the technical architecture of the API platform. An API platform provides an infrastructure for developing, running and managing APIs.

API architecture may refer to the architecture of the API portfolio. When building, running and exposing not only one, but several APIs, it becomes clear that certain building blocks of the API, runtime functionality and management functionality for the API need to be used over and over again. The API portfolio contains all APIs of the enterprise and needs to be managed like its product. API portfolio architecture analyzes the functionality of the API and organizes, manages and reuses the APIs.

API architecture may refer to the design decisions for a particular API proxy. To document the design decisions, API description languages are used (RAML and Swagger).

This book covers all of the above perspectives on API architecture. Which one are you interested in? Jump to the respective chapter.

How to put API Architecture into Practice?

To become useful, the API architecture needs to be put into practice. This is why this book covers an API methodology for design and development. An API methodology provides practical guidelines and explains how to develop an API architecture into an API that consumers love.

The methodology we propose is an outside-in approach, which also incorporates ideas of contract first design and simulation. In this methodology, the contract is expressed in the form of an API description.

In each phase of the methodology, an API description is either created, refined or used: the API description is the red thread connecting all the steps of the methodology.

Why is API Architecture Important?

It is very hard to move the pillar of a bridge, which is made of steel and concrete. Such changes are difficult, costly and time intensive. This is why a blueprint is created before building the bridge. It allows planning all the details, iterating over several proposals and performing what-if analysis. Changes to the plan are easy and cheap to perform. And by making changes to the plan, it hopefully becomes unnecessary to make changes to the real artifacts. The same is true for APIs.

When APIs have already been built, changes are difficult, expensive and time-intensive. Even worse, the changes to published APIs might break any clients using the API. The consumers might get upset and switch the API provider. To avoid this, the API needs to be right from the start, by the first time it is published.

This can be achieved by planning ahead with an API architecture. An appropriate API architecture increases the efficiency of building the right API, reduces the cost and time for both construction and maintenance and thus reduces technical risk associated with the construction.

An API architecture is an approach for risk mitigation. It enforces that the approach is well thought out before construction is started. It avoids situations, in which resources are spent on implementing APIs, which cannot possibly fly.

An appropriate API architecture enables a contract-first design approach. Once the architecture is externalized and written down, it can be used not only by the API providers to implement the API proxy, but also by API consumers to build apps with this API. The API consumer does not have to wait for the API to be finished, but development of API and app can proceed in parallel.

Non-functional properties of the API should not be an afterthought. The API needs to be designed right from the start to fulfill all non-functional properties such as security, performance, availability. Based on an architecture, the implications of the architectural choices on non-functional properties can be determined early in the design.

Proper architecture and design of the APIs is an investment. In the long run, it will save time and even help avoiding mistakes.

API Solution Architecture

To understand the demands and requirements on APIs, let us first study some typical solutions that are enabled by APIs, such as cloud services, mobile apps, multi-channel and omni-channel solutions, web applications and the internet of things.

API solutions typically consist of two types of components. One type of component exposes the APIs and another type of component consumes the APIs. The exposed APIs reside server-side, e.g. in the cloud or on premise. The clients are the API-consuming components. They are typically apps for mobile phones, web browsers or embedded devices for the internet of things. The clients use APIs for connecting to centrally deployed data sources or services in company backends.

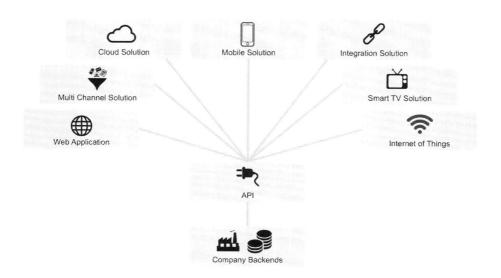

Types of API Solutions

A number of solutions use APIs as their backbone. In the following we study some typical example of solutions that are built with APIs.

Mobile Solutions

The number of mobile and tablet devices has outgrown the number of stationary computers. Mobile apps are different than traditional desktop applications, since most mobile apps are neither autonomous nor self-sufficient. Apps need to connect to the servers on the internet to be usable at all or at least to be usable to their full potential.

The mobile app itself is for the most part just a pretty frontend and user interface. Some business logic will be executed on the mobile, but most heavy processing will happen on servers in the cloud or in the remote data center of the company. The functionality hosted on these servers can be reached via APIs. Also, the data is located on the server-side backends and pulled via API calls. The user data that is gathered by the sensors of the mobile device and the data that is entered by the user is usually sent to APIs on the server, which hand the data to services or directly to data bases.

The data delivered by APIs needs to be lightweight, and partitioned. This ensures that the API can be consumed by devices with limited processing power and limited internet connection bandwidth.

Who provides the APIs used in mobile apps? Some APIs, namely the APIs used for the core functionality of the mobile app, are typically also provided by the providers of mobile apps. More generic APIs are typically provided by third party API providers.

Cloud Solutions

SaaS cloud solutions typically consist of a web application and APIs. The web application is visible for the consumers. Under the hood, cloud solutions usually offer an API as well, however, the API typically remains under the surface. This API can be used for connecting the cloud application with other cloud applications to realize automation or for connecting the cloud solution with mobile apps and desktop software.

Dropbox is an example for this type of cloud solution. The API of this cloud solution allows many third party applications to connect to Dropbox, including synchronization tools for mobile and desktop.

Web Solutions

Web applications display dynamic web pages. Based on the users' requests, the web pages are created on the fly with the data available from the backend. The data displayed on the web pages can be served by APIs. The web application pulls the raw data from APIs, processes the data and displays it on HTML pages.

An e-commerce web application for example displays products on a web site based on the customer's search criteria. The product data is served by the product API, which fetches the product data from a database and returns relevant fields in the form of a JSON structure. The web application interprets the JSON structure and transforms it into an HTML page.

What is the advantage of this architecture? The API can be accessible to other clients, such as a mobile app for integration with a partner, or for a third party app. The web application is just another client of the API. Only one interface needs to be maintained. When appropriate security mechanisms are in place, it can be used by everyone, internally in the organization and externally. It can even be made available to partners or third party developers. A precondition for such an approach is a good security architecture.

Integration Solutions

Businesses are run by software. Industrial production processes are controlled by software. Machines, cars and many consumer products contain software. By integrating businesses, machines or products with other systems, they can become much more powerful and practical. But how does this integration work?

APIs provide the capabilities, which are essential for connecting, extending and integrating software. By integrating software, APIs connect businesses with other businesses. They are used in business to business integration solutions. The business of an enterprise can be expanded by linking the business to partners up and down the value chain. Since businesses are run by IT, the businesses can be better linked by integrating the IT systems of a business up and down the value chain to the IT systems of other businesses, partners, employees and of course to customers.

Integration does not only make sense in a business to business context, often the integration of internal systems, the various systems of an organization, is done prior to any external integration.

Multi-Channel Solutions

Today, e-commerce systems offer customers to shop on several platforms: on the mobile, on the web or on the tablet. However, when customers want to switch from one device to the next one, their shopping cart does not follow along. This is inconvenient for the end-user and may lead to a lost sales opportunity for the shop owner.

To improve the shopping experience, the same data and user actions need to be available on all of the user's devices, even though they are built on different hardware, run different operating systems, and different apps. For the user, it should be a seamless switch from one device to the next one. Omni-channel solutions or multi-channel solutions deliver exactly this. No matter which channel is used by the customers, they get a consistent experience on all their devices and can easily switch between devices.

The architecture ensures that data is stored independently of a particular device or app. Relevant data is stored on a server and made accessible by an API. All devices and apps can connect to the same API, which not only keeps the data but also the "state" information in one single, central location. Since APIs are loosely coupled to their client and do not require complicated, proprietary infrastructure on the side of the client, they are well-suited for this task. In fact, APIs only require the lowest common denominator of all platforms - HTTP access.

Smart TV Solutions

TV is still the most popular medium. Thus it allows content providers and advertisers to reach a large number of people. However, it only allows for one-way communication, the back-channel is missing. This means that the TV company can send its content, but the audience cannot interact, reply or provide feedback in any way.

Smart TV provides a solution. It does not just offer more TV channels, but provides more capabilities for interaction. The back channel for the TV is provided by apps running on the Smart TV. These apps can perform API calls to provide feedback of the audience to the broadcaster.

Internet of Things

The internet of things is made up of physical devices with an internet connection. The devices are controlled by software via their actors or the devices can collect data via their sensors. So the device itself does not need to be "smart", however, it can behave like a smart device. The device connects to smart functions, which are exposed on the internet via APIs. Examples of such API solutions include smart wearables, smart cars, smart homes or smart cities.

Several APIs may be involved in an internet of things solution. Some APIs are deployed in the cloud and receive the data, which was collected by the sensors of the physical device. Other APIs are realized on the device itself and expose the actors of the device.

Software, which is not necessarily running on the device itself can deliver the smart functions and implement the "brain". It analyzes the collected sensor data and sends appropriate commands to the actors on the device via API calls. APIs are the glue. They connect smart functions via the internet with the "things".

In summary, APIs have two functions in the internet of things. APIs are the "call center", which receives all the calls from the devices for leaving their sensor data. APIs are also the "remote control" for steering the devices from a distance.

Stakeholders in API Solutions

There are three main groups of stakeholders for API solutions: API providers develop, design, deploy and manage APIs. API consumers build API solutions, API clients, apps or smart devices using APIs. End users buy and use apps. Note, that the end users do not call the API directly. Instead, end users call the API indirectly via an app.

API Providers

API providers build and expose APIs. They need to know how APIs are designed, built and operated. API providers originate from many diverse industries and form a quite diverse group. Their approach to API architecture may vary, not depending on the industry, but depending on the legacy systems of the enterprise. Some companies have many legacy systems to deal with, others have none.

There are API providers, which are born as API providers. They do not have any legacy systems, yet, which need to be integrated. Examples are Facebook and Twitter. Any functionality these young companies would like to expose, they expose in the form of an API. These companies can start building APIs on the green field. Any new system they build will have APIs from the beginning.

There are also API providers, which start out as traditional enterprises and grow into the API provider role. They have to deal with many legacy systems, which already cover the core functionality of the business. However, these systems are complicated, not user-friendly and cannot be exposed to anyone outside the enterprise. The API does not need to implement the required business functionality, since it is already realized by the existing legacy systems. Instead, the API connects to the backend systems on the one side and to the API consumers on the other side. The API hides the complicated interfaces of the legacy system, but at the same time it uses their functionality.

The business of API providers is the development of APIs for consumers. API providers usually cannot influence the API solutions, which are built with their APIs, but they need to know and understand the needs of the API consumers to be able to offer APIs, which are useful for the consumers. API providers define the API portfolio, roadmap and product model.

It is the responsibility of the API provider to decide which functionality should be exposed by an API. Often, the wish is to expose as much functionality as possible, but resource constraints require that the efforts are in some way prioritized. Which API should be realized first? In a solution driven approach, only those APIs are built, which are required by the API consumers to be able to realize their apps and solutions. The API consumers steer the API development. In a top-down approach on the other hand the API provider defines the important APIs from an internal perspective, e.g. from a reusability perspective and thus steers the development of APIs.

API Consumers

API consumers build solutions with the APIs, such as web applications, cloud services, mobile apps or smart devices for the internet of things. To become API consumers, the developers of the API consumer need to understand how to build an API client, i.e. the component of the API solution that interacts directly with the API. Sometimes, API consumers need to register with the API provider to obtain credentials for accessing the API and its documentation. In addition, API consumers might need to buy a rate plan for accessing monetized APIs.

API providers should always strive to become API consumers of their own APIs. This can be achieved by building a simple app for demonstration purposes. Building a demo app will quickly expose any challenges that other API consumers -- most of all the real API consumers out there -- will have. It is a classic variant of the strategy "eat your own dog food".

End Users

The end user does not call the API directly. Instead, the end user uses the app or web site that was built by the API consumer. This app or website calls the API in the background. However, this happens under the hood and the end user will not notice the API call. The end users will usually not care about the API, see the API, or know that an API is a part of the solution in the first place.

API-related Design Decisions

In the following, a couple of architectural design decisions are discussed, which need to be taken on the level of the solution architecture. They refer to the foundations of the architecture, the allocation of the functionality to either client or server, reusing or building an API or choosing a third party API.

What do all types of API solutions have in common?

API solutions can be built for very diverse use cases. But all API solutions are distributed systems, consisting of client and server components.

API clients may be mobile apps, cloud apps or web applications. These clients provide the user interface for user engagement.

APIs take on the role of the server in the distributed system and thus operate under the hood, invisible for the end users. APIs provide data and services, which are relevant in the context of the solution. For example, they encapsulate the business logic and the storage systems. The API is the entry point to the functionality offered by the enterprise. It is the first and in fact the only system that an API consumer would contact directly.

Functionality in the Client or in the API?

Despite great app development frameworks, not all functionality can be realized inside the app. Typical functionality that cannot be realized inside the app includes:

- Heavy computation or number crunching

- Persistent storage of data

- Storage across several devices for realizing omni-channel experiences

- Storage of sensitive data

- Access to real time data

Since the above functionality cannot be provided by the client, it is typically realized on the server and exposed in the form of an API. The client merely connects to the API.

Use an existing API or build a new API?

The design of the API client includes the choice of the API. The API consumer has the choice to use an existing API (and pay for its use) or to build a new API. When given the choice, API consumers typically prefer to just use an API that has already been developed and tested. This allows API consumers to integrate the API quickly and focus on adding value on top with their app.

If the required API already exists, the API client can be built quickly. The API consumer needs to register the new client with the API provider to receive credentials, set up the payment for the usage of the API and integrate the API with the client. The important steps for choosing a third party API are outlined in the next section.

More often, however, none of the existing APIs fits the requirements exactly. A completely new API may need to be developed. The API may be developed by a third party API provider or by an API consumer. If the API is developed by the API consumer, the API consumer also becomes an API provider. The important steps for building APIs are described in the rest of the book.

How to choose a third party API?

When integrating a third party API, the API consumer needs to be able to (1) find this API, (2) learn about the API, (3) test the API and (4) use the API. For a quick integration it is essential, that these four steps are as smooth as possible for the API consumer.

Step 1: Find the API

There is a global market for third party APIs. The API consumer can choose from the offers on this market. APIs are typically sold as services, i.e. the API consumer pays for the usage of the API. Various models may be available to pay for the usage, i.e. by the number of calls, number of days, by the bandwidth and many other options.

Step 2: Learn about the API

APIs are essential components of modern apps. The app might even stop working if the API stops working. This is why the API consumer needs to trust the API provider. API consumers may worry about the API provider not being around any longer, the API provider switching off the API or changing the API. This is why API consumers are interested in the stability and longevity of the API. When choosing an API, consumers should evaluate both the stability of the API provider as a company and the stability of the API from a technical perspective.

A hint for the stability of the API provider is a sound business model. Providing APIs needs to make business sense for the provider. This is why paid APIs are typically considered "safer" and more stable. Keeping alive paid APIs is in the self-interest of the API provider, so API provider and API consumer are aligned.

A hint for the stability of the API is provided by the history of the API. Has the API been changed? Are new versions deployed? Are old versions still supported? Is the phase-out at the end of the API life cycle described in the terms of service?

Step 3: Test the API

API consumers typically want to test the API before committing to its use in order to confirm that it satisfies both runtime aspects and development aspects of the overall requirements. Runtime aspects comprise the functional requirements and the non-functional requirements of the API, such as stability, longevity, performance and security. The development aspects comprise the relationship between API provider and the developers of the API consumer.

The development aspect might be more important than it seems, since the developers of the API consumer are in fact the only people who interact with the API directly.

What do the developers of the API consumers look for? API consumers look for APIs with a great community, great support, great documentation and tools that will make client development and operation as smooth and simple as possible. And ideally, the engagement platform makes it easy to get a taste the API via an interactive documentation.

Step 4: Use the API

Documentation and credentials should to be easily available for new consumers. Engagement platforms typically provide generated (potentially interactive) documentation and a self-service interface for obtaining credentials, such as client IDs or API keys.

38

API Platform Architecture

API platforms are used by API providers to realize new APIs efficiently.

New APIs are typically not built from scratch but from the building blocks provided by an API platform. This platform can be anything from a simple JEE platform to a fully-featured API management platform. A platform allows for reuse on several levels and for the efficient development of APIs.

In this chapter we answer typical questions about API platforms, such as: Why do we need an API platform? What is an API platform? Which capabilities does and API platform have? How is an API platform organized? What is the architecture of an API platform? And how does the API platform fit into the surrounding technical architecture of the enterprise?

Overview

Why do we need API platforms? It is certainly technically feasible to build APIs without any platform or framework. But, why would you? For a moment, let's think about databases, which provide us a platform for building applications. You could certainly build your application without a database and write your own data storage library. But we typically do not do that. We use an existing database as a platform. And this is best practice for good reasons. It allows us to focus on building the application that serves the business case, because we can reuse existing, proven components and build the application quicker. The same argumentation applies for API platforms:

API platforms allow us to focus on building APIs that consumers love, since we can reuse existing, proven API building blocks and build APIs quicker.

So what is an API platform? An API platform typically consists of at least the following three platform components:

- API Development Platform: This platform enables API providers to develop APIs quickly and with high quality. It offers API building blocks, which are proven, reusable and configurable. It also offers tools for design and development of APIs.

- API Runtime Platform: This platform primarily executes the APIs. It serves API responses for incoming API requests of the consumers with favorable non-functional properties, such as high throughput and low latency.

- API Engagement Platform: This platform allows API providers to manage their interaction with API consumers. It offers API documentation, credentials and rate plans for API consumers. For API providers it offers product management and configuration capabilities.

In the following sections we answer the question "Which capabilities does each API platform component have?"

API Development Platform

The API development platform offers a toolbox for API design and development. The toolbox contains API building blocks, which are proven, reusable and configurable. APIs are constructed by composing these building blocks. Thus, there is no need to reinvent the wheel for the development of each new API. The API development platform also offers an integrated engineering environment with tools for the efficient design and development of APIs.

The toolbox offered by the development platform consists of:

- Library of API building blocks.
- Language for implementing APIs.
- IDE for API development with editor, debugger and deployment tools.
- Language for designing APIs.
- Design tool for creating API interface designs.

- Tool for generating documentation and code skeletons based on the design.

The API development platform is targeted at the API developers, who work for the API provider. This platform supports the developers and enables them to develop APIs quickly and with high quality.

Library of API Building Blocks

When developing APIs, certain functionality is needed over and over again. It is extremely helpful to have this functionality available in a shared library of building blocks. The building blocks can be reused and do not need to be developed over and over whenever the functionality is needed. The building blocks are tested and proven in practice, so bugs are extremely seldom. The building blocks are configurable and can be adapted for many purposes. The building blocks are composable, i.e. an API can be built from a collection of properly configured building blocks.

The building blocks offered by the development platform span the following features at a minimum:

- Processing of HTTP requests and HTTP responses, including header parameters, query parameters, URI processing, HTTP status code, HTTP methods

- Security: threat protection, IP-based access limitation, location-based access limitation, time-based access limitation

- Frontend authentication and authorization with OAuth, Basic Authorization, API key

- Backend authentication and authorization with SAML, LDAP, XACML

- Frontend protocols: HTTP (REST), SOAP, XML-RPC, JSON-RPC, WebSockets, XMPP, Push Notifications

- Backend protocols: HTTP (REST), SOAP, XML-RPC, JSON-RPC, JMS, RMI, Cloud Services

- Protocol mediation: SOAP to HTTP (REST), HTTP (REST) to SOAP

- Data format transformation: XML to JSON, JSON to XML

- Structural transformation: XSLT, XPath, JSONPath

- Data integrity and protection: encryption and signing

- Routing to one or multiple backends

- Aggregation and orchestration of multiple APIs and/or multiple backend services

- Throttling to protect your backends: rate limitation and throughput limitation

- Throttling to protect the API platform: rate limitation and throughput limitation

- Load balancing for incoming requests to the API platform and outgoing requests to the backends

- Cache for incoming requests to the API platform and outgoing requests to the backends

- Hooks for logging

- Hooks for analytics

- Monetization capabilities

Language for Implementing APIs

The building blocks presented in the previous section need to be composed to form an API. Typically, a language is used for composing the building blocks. This language can be either a general purpose programming language or a domain-specific API development language.

General purpose programming languages such as Java or JavaScript have the advantage of wide-spread use and many generic supporting tools. The efficiency of development with general purpose languages can be improved by frameworks such as Node.js or Express.js for JavaScript and JAX-RS, Jersey, Restlet or Spring for Java.

API development languages are domain-specific configuration languages. They intentionally limit the expressibility. API development languages only offer a handful of language constructs, but all of them are relevant for API development. This intentional and focused limitation is an advantage, since it is easier to learn them, easier to understand them and easier to validate them to discover erroneous or missing configurations. They offer the advantage that APIs can be built by pure configuration, resulting in much smaller, more compact and more understandable implementations. API development languages usually offer their own integrated development environment with editor, compiler, debugger and deployment capabilities. DSLs are typically linked with a specific API development platform and are product-specific.

Besides the technical reasons for general purpose languages or domain specific languages, the existing skill set of your developers needs to be considered. It is usually more efficient to write APIs in a language that the API developers are familiar with and already productive in.

Language for Designing APIs

Not only the implementation of the API needs to be described, but also the design of the API. This is why API development platforms provide two types of languages: There is a low-level API implementation language and a high-level API description language.

The higher-level language is used for designing APIs and is also called API description language. It is used to express the "what" of APIs. The lower-level language, the API implementation language, is used for implementing APIs and for expressing the "how".

API platforms provide not only the language, but also design tools for creating API interface designs, tools for generating documentation from the API description and tools for generating implementations. If an implementation can be generated from the design, the generated implementations needs to fit with the strategically chosen language for implementation. In a later chapter on API methodology the use of API descriptions in various stages along the development process is detailed.

An API description language is a domain-specific language for expressing API design. The well-defined semantics of the language and the tooling ecosystem are the main advantages of API description languages compared to generic modeling language, such as UML (Unified Modeling Language). In a separate chapter on API description languages we study the capabilities of these languages in depth.

API Runtime Platform

The API runtime platform primarily executes the APIs. It enables the APIs to accept incoming requests from API consumers and to serve responses. The foundation of an API runtime platform is an HTTP server, which allows exposing services via HTTP.

45

The API runtime platform should deliver favorable non-functional properties, such as high stability, high throughput, high availability and high security. To meet the non-functional properties, the platform offers capabilities for load balancing, connection pooling and caching. The runtime platform should also offer capabilities for monitoring, logging and analytics for checking if the desired non-functional properties are met.

The API runtime platform is also responsible for providing capabilities for the smooth deployment of new APIs and the maintenance of existing APIs. It also needs capabilities for credential and configuration management. These features help to keep track of the credentials and configurations for multiple environments and for multiple backend systems.

In summary, the runtime infrastructure provides capabilities for:

- Load balancing, connection pooling and caching

- Monitoring, logging and analytics

- Deployment and maintenance

- Credential and configuration management

API Engagement Platform

An API engagement platform is used by the API provider to interact with its community of API consumers. The platform offers API providers the capabilities of product management and configuration. API providers use the following capabilities of the API engagement platform:

- API management: configuration and reconfiguration of existing APIs without the need for deployment of the API

- API discovery: a mechanism for clients to obtain information about the APIs

- Consumer onboarding (Client ID/App Key generation, Interactive API console)

- Community management (Blogs, Forums, Social features etc.)

- Documentation (Ideally an interactive documentation, which was generated from the API description)

- Version management

- Management of monetization and service level agreements (SLA)

For API consumers, the API engagement platform is the information hub for inspecting the API portfolio, accessing specific API documentation, managing credentials and managing rate plans. From the perspective of the API consumers, the platform offers:

- An overview of the API portfolio

- A source of inspiration for API solutions

- Documentation of APIs

- Possibility to try APIs interactively

- Example source code for integration

- Self service to get access to APIs (credentials and rate plans)

- Service announcements

- Client tooling, such as code generators for clients

API Platform Configurations and Interactions

Environments

Usually, the APIs are not only deployed on a productive system, they need to be deployed on different stages of increasing maturity. The stages are sometimes also called environments. Each of the stages has a specific purpose and is separated from the other stages to isolate potential errors to a single stage. In each of the stages, the deployed APIs are tested and validated.

Typically we find a subset of the following stages, ordered by increasing maturity:

- Simulation: Used for playing with interface design, provide mocks or simulation of an API, allow interaction with consumers (e.g. mobile app developers)

- Development: Used for development, which will eventually go to production

- Continuous Integration: Used for automated testing of the latest version. It is intended to provide feedback on the latest development version with short turnaround times.

- Testing: Used for manual black box testing and integration testing.

- Pre-Production: Used as a practice for production and for acceptance testing.

- Production: Used as a real system for consumers.

The API platform and the surrounding systems should have a very similar setup. Ideally, there is a smooth migration of the API and its configuration from one stage to the next, after all the tests in the previous stage have been completed. In addition, there should be a dashboard, which shows how the API matures from one stage to the next.

The components of the API platform should be available in different environments. Especially the runtime platform and the engagement platform should be available in different environments. Only one instance of the development platform is needed, since it can be shared among all environments.

API Platform Deployment Models

The API platform may be deployed on premise or in the cloud.

Most API platforms are on premise solutions, since the required backend systems are also on premise. For security reasons the backend systems should not be available via the internet. The API layer is an additional protection and security layer for the backend systems.

API platforms, which are available in the cloud, are typically elastic and scale well. API platforms in the cloud make sense, if they do not need to connect to secured backend systems in a private network. This is for example the case, if the backends of the APIs are publicly available services or APIs on other cloud systems. One possibility for connecting to backend systems out of an API platform in the cloud, would be a connection via VPN (virtual private network).

Interactions between the Platforms

In the previous section we have introduced the purpose, structure and behavior of the three API platform components. Typically, these three components are used together and there are some dependencies between the platform components. We study the relations between these components and answer the questions: How do the platform components relate? And which tasks are necessary to connect the platform components?

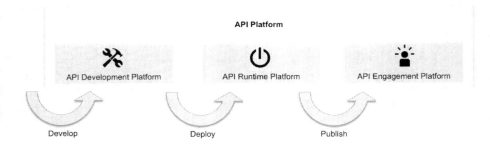

Design and Development

Design and development activity is only performed on the development platform. It does not affect any other platform.

Deployment

When the development of an API proxy is finished, it is ready for deployment. Deployment transfers the API proxy (in a compiled or interpretable format) from the development platform to the runtime platform. Configurations and credentials need to be available on the runtime platform. All the building block libraries and external dependencies are expected to be available on the runtime platform. Note, that the API proxy is not available for consumers directly after the initial deployment.

Publishing

An API proxy that has been deployed for the first time, needs to be published. Only published API proxies are available on the engagement platform and on the runtime platform. Once published, the API is listed in the portfolio of the engagement platform, its documentation is generated from the API description, overall monitoring and analytics are started for the API.

During publication, the authentication and authorization parameters for the API proxy are configured, so the API proxy becomes properly secured, can be monitored and monetized on a per consumer basis.

Surrounding Systems

The API platform is not an isolated system, but it needs to be integrated into the existing architecture of the enterprise. In this chapter we study the interfaces between the API platform and other architectural building blocks of the technical architecture.

The size and complexity of the architecture surrounding the API platform typically depend on the size of the company. Large enterprises have many legacy systems. They have grown their architecture organically and their architecture is full of special cases. The technical architecture of an enterprise is complex and thus the API platform becomes complex, requiring many and diverse interfaces to other building blocks. Small startups typically have no legacy systems and can form their architecture around the API platform. Some of the building blocks presented in the following may not even exist in a startup since they are not necessary, leading to a simpler technical architecture.

API clients are outside the scope of the surrounding systems of the API platform. Consumers develop clients to access the APIs. Clients can be mobile apps, web applications, cloud services or embedded devices for the internet of things.

The surrounding systems are partly before the API platform, i.e. between the clients and the API platform and partly they are hidden behind the API platform. Before the API platform, there are typically firewalls to improve the security and load balancers to improve the performance. Behind the API platform there are IAM systems for managing identity information and backend systems for providing the core functionality of the enterprise.

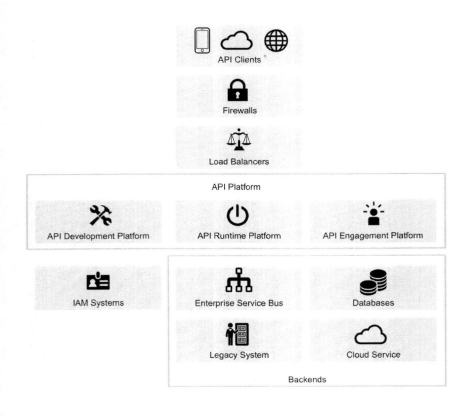

Load Balancers and Firewalls

Security devices are usually placed between the internet and the API platform. IP level filtering (ISO/OSI level 3) is typically performed by a separate security device, while application level filtering (ISO/OSI level 7) is performed by the API runtime platform.

Load balancers are usually placed between the API platform and the internet. Some API platforms may offer load balancing capabilities out of the box, others may rely on external components. They are used to route the traffic from the internet to one of several nodes of an API platform running as a cluster. The load balancer spreads the requests equally among the nodes.

Another place for load balancers is between the API platform and the backend system. The API platform sends all requests for a specific backend system to a load balancer, which balances the requests over several instances of the backend system.

Identity and Access Management Infrastructure

In its position on the fringes of the enterprise IT system, APIs need to authenticate and authorize the users. This is why the API platform should provide building blocks for authentication and authorization.

To be able to offer OAuth, OpenID Connect and social login, an OAuth provider and an OpenID Connect provider are typically part of the runtime platform. At the same time, the existing identity and access management infrastructure needs to be reused as much as possible. The API platform needs to connect to existing identity stores such as LDAP or Active Directory and to existing authentication and authorization systems.

Which components of the platform need identity information? The development platform needs the identities of the developers. The engagement platform needs the identities of consumers. The runtime platform needs the identities of consumers, and potentially also end users and developers.

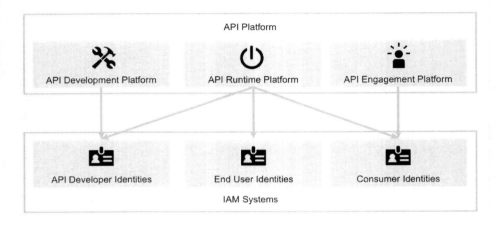

Existing Functionality in Backends

APIs typically do not implement the core business logic of the enterprise, nor do they store customer or business data. However, APIs need to have access to this data and the business services.

The data and services typically reside in backend systems. Backend systems form the heart of the enterprise. Due to their vital role, backends need to be protected, both from a security perspective and from a performance & availability perspective. It is the responsibility of the API platform to secure the access to the backend system and to limit the load on the backends to a healthy and manageable level.

Backend systems typically do not provide the data and services in an easily digestible form. Data and services that are offered by backend systems are typically big, ugly, complicated, not easily digestible and simply not customer-friendly. The backends do contain valuable information, but the relevant information is typically buried deep inside the data, and relevant functionality is spread out over several services on different systems. It is the responsibility of the API to aggregate, filter and process the data into an easily-consumable form.

Enterprises typically have a large set of backend systems using a variety of technologies. Backends may be databases, applications, enterprise service buses or web services using SOAP interfaces, REST interfaces, or message queues. The data is available in XML or proprietary formats. It is the responsibility of the API to offer the data and services in a homogeneous, modern protocol and data format.

Credentials, URIs and further connection details for the different deployment environments need to be available in the configuration management database of the runtime platform. In addition, IP-level firewall rules need to allow the connections from the runtime platform to the respective backends.

New Functionality

API proxies only expose existing functionality and protect it. New business logic should not be realized on the API platform directly. Instead, it should be realized on a backend system. However, the technology and data format for newly constructed backend systems can already conform to the requirements of the externally facing API proxy.

Enterprise Service Buses and SOA Platforms

Many enterprises already have a SOA platform such as an Enterprise Service Bus. You might ask yourself why you cannot use a SOA platform for exposing APIs. Indeed, there are similarities, especially when looking some of the basic functionality of the products, such as proxies, message transformation and security. However, there are also important differences, which might render SOA platforms insufficient or at least inconvenient for exposing APIs. In this section we will explain the differences between the SOA approach and the API approach.

SOA solutions are designed and built by the service provider. The consumers are typically in the same organization. The management of the organization orders all departments of the organization to consume the newly created service. Due to this organizational structure, the opinion of the service consumer about the service does not matter so much in SOA. The organizational structure ensures, that for every service built, there is a guaranteed consumer in a SOA environment.

For APIs, the situation is different. The consumers are outside the company of the API provider. There is no instance that can dictate the use of the newly built API. API consumers only choose to use the API, if it makes sense for them. API consumers can typically choose from a set of APIs that offer similar functionality. If the API is in some way difficult to consume, API consumers can just move on to the next API offered by a different API provider. There is no guaranteed consumer for any given API and competition is much tougher.

The well-known SOA principles, however, still apply to APIs. These principles are service orientation, reuse, separation of concerns and loose coupling. SOA promised external integration outside the organization, but this aspect was not widely adopted. APIs are another attempt for supporting external integration, using a different technological stack. APIs are simply a specialized version of web services, and provide similar technical benefits. Today, there is a place for both SOA services and APIs. A SOA service is preferred, when sharing functionality within the organization. An API is preferred for sharing functionality with several consumers outside the organization.

It might be tempting to open up some of the internal SOA services to partners and to expose internal SOA services in the form of APIs. However, internal services are often not very consumer-friendly. They are usually very complex and include a lot of details, which are irrelevant for the external consumer. This is why internal services cannot be exposed one to one as APIs. The external API interface needs to be designed based on consumer preferences. The implementation of the API typically includes a mapping from internal to external interface.

API Portfolio Architecture

Usually, an organization does not only have a single API proxy, but several API proxies. Together, all these API proxies form the API portfolio of the organization. The API portfolio should, however, be more than a haphazard collection of whatever APIs were found in the organization. The API portfolio should be a consciously designed product and all the APIs in the portfolio need to be consistent with each other, reusable, discoverable and customizable.

Requirements

API portfolio design is a concern for different API stakeholders. Both API consumers and API providers have significant advantages from a properly designed API portfolio and both parties formulate requirements for the API portfolio regarding consistency, reuse, customization, discoverability and longevity. In the following subsections, we study these requirements in more detail. Solutions satisfying these requirements are provided later, in the section on governance.

Consistency

An API solution, such as a mobile app, may use several API proxies from the portfolio and the output of one API is the input to the next API.

From the API consumer's perspective, it is important that the APIs harmonize well when used together and are consistent with each other. Consistency is required regarding data structures, representations, URIs, error messages and the behavior of the APIs. API consumers find it easier to learn about and work with an API, if it behaves similar to the last one and delivers the similar error messages.

From an API provider's perspective, managing a consistent portfolio is easier than managing a portfolio without structure. A consistent portfolio contains many commonalities among the APIs. These commonalities can be factored out, shared and reused. In the end, this reuse leads to a speed-up in the development. By reusing common elements, the wheel is not reinvented each time a new API is built. Instead a common library of patterns and know-how is shared and reused. This leads to the next step: reuse of implementations and designs among APIs.

Reuse

Developing a new API is a project that binds resources of the API provider. Such a project should only be started if the resulting API can likely be used and reused by many apps and in many API solutions. This is why API portfolio design needs to produce reusable APIs. Reuse can be realized in several ways: reuse of the API by several apps, reuse of the API by multiple APIs, or reuse of parts of the API.

APIs should not be developed for specific consumers -- APIs should always be used by several consumers, solutions or projects. APIs can be used by apps, but they can also be used by other APIs. In this case, APIs become the building blocks for bigger APIs and are thus reused.

If not the complete API can be reused, at least a part of the API could be reused. Common functionality can be factored out into shared libraries and the shared libraries are reused. The reuse and the consistency requirement go hand in hand and lead to the same results.

Customization

A successful API portfolio addresses and satisfies the needs of its API consumers. When an API portfolio is newly designed or extended, the consumers' needs and expectations have to be considered. But what happens if the consumers are not a homogeneous group and they have little in common? What if each consumer has different requirements for the APIs?

In this case, the one size fits all approach for APIs does not provide adequate results. The proposed alternative is a customization approach, which ensures that each consumer can get APIs which match the consumer's individual need.

But ... in the above section on reuse we claimed that no APIs should be developed for a specific API consumers and in this section we claim that APIs should be customized for each consumer. A contradiction? No, we claim that both can be realized at the same time.

Discoverability

To expand the usage of APIs, it should be easy for an API consumer to find and discover all APIs in the API portfolio. API portfolio design needs to ensure that APIs can be found and all the information that is necessary for the proper usage is available.

Longevity

Longevity means that important aspects of a software do not change and stay stable for a long time. This might be a surprising requirement in an environment, where everything is agile and the mantra is "release early and release often". What needs to stay stable is the signature of the API, the client facing interface. The reason for this requirement is that typically many consumers rely on an API and changes in the signature would break the consumers. This is especially the case, when clients are not software clients, but are hardware devices, e.g. for the Internet of Things. These devices often contain hardcoded URIs and parameters for API calls. In addition these devices often have no software-update functionality. This is not because of bad engineering practice, but rather because of the stringent resource limitations of the devices. In this chapter we study techniques for obtaining longevity, namely change management and versioning approaches.

Governance

We have identified consistency, reuse, customization and discoverability as the main requirements for API portfolio design. In the remainder of this chapter we provide solution patterns for these requirements. These requirements for the API portfolio, which were identified in the last section, scream for governance processes.

An API initiative is often regarded as the innovation lab of an enterprise. To fulfill this vision, the API portfolio should inspire, spark creativity and enable the enterprise to build innovative apps with little effort. The idea of governance for APIs and the rigid rules, which are associated with governance processes, might seem to be in conflict with the idea of APIs as a lightweight innovation lab. However, governance for APIs has its place in the API portfolio management. If done right, governance does not need to create heavy processes that suppress innovation. Instead, API governance of the API portfolio is realized in a lean and lightweight fashion.

To manage the conflicting requirements of governance and agility, the portfolio may actually be split into two separate API portfolios: One portfolio is dedicated to innovative and experimental APIs, which are not in productive use, yet. This portfolio can be developed without any restricting governance rules. Another portfolio is dedicated to stable, productive APIs, which are offered to external API consumers. Only this last portfolio of productive APIs is required to follow a lightweight governance process.

Consistency

Consistency may focus on internal development guidelines, which are only relevant for the developers of the API providers. On the other side, consistency may be focused around the externally visible interface definitions, which are relevant for API consumers. No matter which scope is chosen for the consistency, a set of rules are defined that can be used for consistency checks. Each enterprise may implement its own set of consistency rules. Such rules make it easy to ensure consistency among all the APIs in the portfolio, compliance with company standards, and the appropriate level of protection, security and privacy.

Consistency rules may include some of the following points:

- The URI for the APIs should follow a common structure and should be intuitive. This includes the use of path parameters and query parameters.

- Resources and representations should follow a common structure. If the representations of different APIs share data fields, the names of the data fields and the format in which the data is presented should be consistent across all APIs in the portfolio.

- Common patterns should be factored out and reused consistently by all APIs in the portfolio.

- Input validation rules should be applied consistently across all APIs in the portfolio.

- The same selection of security mechanisms should be applied consistently across all APIs in the portfolio. For the OAuth security mechanism, grant types and scopes should be used consistently. Especially the naming and the semantics of the scopes should be consistent.

More rules for API design and specifically RESTful API design are explained in detail in the API University book on API Design [30].

Consistency Checks in Practice

When the consistency rules are defined, consistency checks can be realized as either a manual or as an automated process. A lightweight consistency check can be realized by setting up some manual quality checks or reviews performed by colleagues.

An alternative to manual checking is automated checking, which can be executed periodically or event-triggered. These automated checks are based on syntactic rules, which are typically much more restrictive and precise than the rules used for manual checking. A complementary approach is the automated code generation based on an API description. It helps developers to get started with a code skeleton, which is conform to the API description. However, this does not necessarily ensure that the implementation is still conform to the API description at the end of the development phase. Mechanisms for ensuring reuse and consistency are discussed in the sections on reuse and consistency, respectively.

Reuse

To identify reuse potential within an API portfolio, system thinking is needed rather than a one-off thought process. This can be achieved by first identifying possible usage scenarios, which contain more than one API. Such usage scenarios can exemplify the different ways in which APIs can be combined with each other and how APIs need to be connected. This is more important than defining a single API specification.

Reuse can be applied on different levels of granularity, depending on the requirements. On whichever level reuse is applied, it always contributes to the consistency of the portfolio.

Reuse of API Features

On the first level, there are reusable building blocks, which are offered by the development platform (see chapter on platform architecture).

These building blocks ensure e.g. HTTP and OAuth standard conformity. To form an API, these building blocks can be configured and composed using an API implementation language.

On the next level, there are reusable solution patterns, which can be realized as compositions of building blocks. They can be offered in the form of provider-specific libraries. Provider-specific libraries are typically used for ensuring company-wide consistency. An example is API fault handling, which needs to produce errors with specific error codes and error messages.

Reuse of Complete APIs

On a larger scale, complete APIs can be reused. In fact, all APIs should be used by several API consumers and in different API solutions. APIs should not be built for one consumer only. Apart from the reuse by consumers, APIs can also be reused by other APIs. In this case, APIs become the building blocks for new APIs. New APIs can be composed of reusable APIs by aggregating or orchestrating them. Furthermore, these reusable APIs can be configured according to the preferences of each API consumer.

If APIs are developed without portfolio design, multiple APIs are created with roughly the same content for different projects, a lot of rework is done and similar API proxies are built with a large engineering effort. A typical starting point for organizations is a project based organization, that defines the need for new APIs.

Reusing own APIs

From an API consumer's perspective there are "own" APIs, and "third party" APIs. Own APIs are developed by the same organization as the app; the API consumer is also the API provider.

A typical pattern is an API calling another API on the same platform. This pattern is applied for decorating the original API with an additional input validation or with additional security checks. Composing APIs from other APIs is studied in the chapter API portfolio architecture.

Depending on the capabilities of the platform, the request can be either routed via the TCP stack, or via a local function call. If the request is routed via TCP, it can either go to the local instance or via the load balancer on the next free instance. If the API platform supports the optimization to route API calls via local function calls, this alternative is recommended.

Reusing Third-Party APIs

While the actual API call might be similar for third party APIs and own APIs, a couple of aspects might be different between the two.

Own APIs are typically used for exposing data from an internal backend service. Alternatively an API may also be used for re-exposing third party APIs. This makes sense, if the new API adds some value, or assimilates the API to the rest of the portfolio. This can be achieved by adapting the data formats used in the original APIs, unifying the security mechanisms used, enriching the exposed data, aggregating the data from multiple APIs, filtering the data or improving the availability & performance of the original API by caching.

A critical aspect is the adaptation of the security mechanisms that is used for protecting the API. Each organization offering a third-party API used in the same app, potentially has its own OAuth provider and only accepts OAuth tokens created by their own OAuth provider. This is why the app connecting to own and third-party APIs or apps connecting to multiple third-party APIs needs to hold multiple OAuth tokens.

67

A solution for this situation can be provided by changing all third-party APIs used in an app to own APIs. This can be accomplished by creating forwarding API proxies on the own API management platform. For each third-party API, there is a proxy on the own platform. An advantage of this approach is the homogeneous API portfolio and homogeneous security and access control from the perspective of the API consumer. As a result, the same security and access control applies to all APIs, whether the APIs are internal or external.

There may be legal restrictions for re-exposing third party APIs. To find out whether it is allowed to reuse third party APIs, check their terms of service.

Customization

A successful API portfolio addresses and satisfies the needs of the API consumers. The APIs and the API portfolio as a whole are built to satisfy primarily the needs of the API consumers and only secondarily the needs of the API provider. This however, assumes that the consumers and their needs are a homogeneous group. Is this a realistic assumption? What if the consumers have little in common and each consumer has different requirements for the APIs? As it turns out, each consumer has different needs and requirements: for a given API, some consumers might expect an elaborate response with many data fields, while others need only one field and thus prefer a fast and lightweight API that does not require additional processing time for the extra fields in the response.

But ... In the above section on reuse we claimed that no APIs should be developed for a specific API consumers and in this section, we claim that APIs should be customized for each consumer. A contradiction? How can the API portfolio be consumer-centric if each and every consumer has different expectations regarding the selection of APIs in the API portfolio and the functionality of each API? Do we need to build separate APIs for the different consumer needs? Would it be economical to build a separate API for each API consumer?

In this case, the one-size-fits-all approach for APIs is not adequate. But from an economical perspective, it is equally inadequate to build individual APIs for each consumer.

One viable solution is a customization approach. By customizing certain aspects of the API, each consumer can obtain APIs matching their individual needs. But which aspects of the API should be customized? Before we get into the details of the customization approach, we first identify the most relevant aspects for customization.

APIs typically cover the following three aspects:

- Data Formatting: APIs need to format the data, prune irrelevant or unnecessary data elements, transform data structures and data values, perform additional lookups to enrich the data, perform caching and perform some fault tolerance mechanisms, such as retries for missing elements.

- Data Delivery: APIs need to serve the data using an appropriate protocol and format the resources and representations appropriately.

- Data Gathering: APIs need to collect the data they expose from one or several backends.

Let us try to find out, which stakeholder is mostly concerned with which aspect of APIs. If we knew which aspect is important for API consumers, we would know the aspects that need to be customized. All other aspects of the API can remain static for all consumers.

69

Which stakeholder cares most about data gathering? The API consumers are not concerned about data gathering, they just want to use the API. The API provider, however is very interested in data gathering, which backends to use, how they deliver the data and which firewalls need to be opened.

Which stakeholder cares most about data formatting and data delivery? The API provider usually does not have any preferences regarding formatting or protocol, as long as it is supported by the API platform. The API consumer, however, is typically very interested in the format of the data, its structure and the degree of detail of the delivered data.

Approach

We now know that the API consumer is interested in data formatting and data delivery. Different API consumers will need their data formatted and delivered in different ways. Data formatting and data delivery need to be customizable. Data gathering, however, is no concern for the API consumer. It requires only one solution, which is used uniformly by all API consumers.

Since data formatting and data delivery are only interesting for API consumers and data gathering is only interesting for the API provider, it makes sense to separate these concerns into two separate APIs. One API, we call it the utility API, only covers the data gathering aspect. The other API, we call it the consumer API, performs only data delivery and data formatting according to the customized needs of the consumer.

Consumer APIs: As their name suggests, consumer APIs can be customized according to the needs of specific API consumers. Consumer APIs use utility APIs. A consumer API orchestrates and filters the results of a number of utility APIs. Utility APIs are the building blocks used for composing consumer APIs. The consumer API can be customized, especially the data formatting and data delivery aspects of the consumer API.

Utility APIs: Utility APIs perform the data gathering from the backends. Utility APIs are internal APIs, meaning that they cannot be called by consumers directly. Instead, these APIs can only be called by consumer APIs or by other utility APIs. Generic APIs are typical realized as utility APIs.

It is not necessary to build an individual consumer API for each consumer. Instead, one instance of a consumer API is sufficient, which can be customized by a configuration. How are consumer APIs configured? The configuration of the APIs is performed by the provider. For each API consumer a configuration package is created. The configuration is saved on the API platform. The configuration typically contains a filter specification for the API response, i.e. which fields are included and a selection of the security mechanism used for a specific consumer.

Summary

This approach ensures that APIs can be systematically customized and reused and no individual and special versions of the APIs need to be built. Project-specific variants of a consumer API can be created, by adapting the configuration of the consumer API.

Discoverability

Discovery is about making it as easy as possible for the API consumer to find the APIs in the portfolio. We mainly distinguish manual and automated discovery. Manual discovery is the dominant strategy and automated discovery is mainly a topic for the future.

Manual Discovery

The discovery of APIs is typically a manual process: API consumers may discover APIs with the help of API catalogues and API yellow pages (such as www.programmableweb.com). These catalogues sort APIs by topic, for example by the topics payment, fitness or social. The catalogs offer search functionality, so API consumers can quickly find the API for the challenges they are facing.

However, several APIs are typically listed for each topic or search word. The API consumers may discover each API further based on the documentation on the provider's engagement platform. Having a great API is usually not enough to drive API uptake, it is however a precondition. Word of mouth works great for APIs. But due to the typical manual discovery approach of consumers, it is very important for API providers to list their APIs and especially new APIs in API catalogs and to create an attractive engagement platform for them.

Automated Discovery

Besides manual discovery, there is the possibility for automated API discovery. While manual discovery is performed by developers, automated discovery is performed by software. For SOAP based services, automated discovery has been standardized by WSDL and UDDI. The automated discovery of APIs is not as institutionalized as for SOAP-based services, yet. There is no agreed-upon format for meta-information about APIs. But with API descriptions, one can obtain automated discovery functionality close to what is offered by SOAP services.

To realize automated discovery, the API description of the API portfolio needs to be served to the consumer. The API consumer needs to be able to parse and interpret the API description. From there on, the consumer should have the information, which is necessary to use the API. This idea can be implemented in various ways, since no standard has been established, yet.

For example, there may be an API that serves the API descriptions for all APIs in the portfolio. The URI of that API would be enough for the API consumer to be able to discover the whole API portfolio.

Alternatively, each API might offer a resource, which serves the API description. This approach is similar to the WSDL approach, where attaching the query parameter ?wsdl to the URI of the service, serves a description of the service for discovery.

Another alternative approach is offered by HTTP. It offers a standardized interface but only limited functionality. HTTP offers the OPTIONS method, which enables discovery of the allowed HTTP methods on a per-resource basis. However, it does not include discovery on an API or portfolio basis, and it neither includes a description of the parameters nor a description of request and response.

Change Management and Versioning

> "Successful software always gets changed."
> -- Frederick P. Brooks

Managing change in software systems is never easy, but it is especially difficult to manage change in loosely-coupled, distributed systems, such as API solutions. In loosely-coupled distributed systems not only the software components themselves are distributed, but also the responsibilities of the different components are distributed.

The Evolution Challenge

If the interface of the API changes, it is clear that the implementation of the API needs to be adapted. It is also clear, that all clients (i.e. apps) relying on the API need to be adapted accordingly. This is simple, if the interface provider is in charge of the clients which have access to the interface. In case the interface changes, the interface provider can trigger that the appropriate changes are made in all clients. This is, however, not the case for APIs.

APIs have published interfaces. Published interfaces are available for anyone to read and study - not only for a selected few. (Even though an API is published, it can be protected by a security mechanisms. Publication and protection are not mutually exclusive.)

The API provider has little control over the implementations done by the consumers and the API provider might not even know all consumers calling the API. The apps are developed by third party developers. The API provider can thus not make appropriate changes in all clients, if the interface changes [18]. If the interface of the API changes, it is impossible for the API provider to change all the apps consuming the API, just as it is impractical to force all consumers to adapt or update their apps, just because the API changed. Consumers are often unwilling or uninterested in dealing with API changes and will quickly abandon any APIs that force them to rewrite their app.

Why does the Evolution Challenge exist at all?

Different forces are at work when publishing interfaces: From an innovation perspective or business perspective, there are forces to publish APIs as early as possible. From an IT governance perspective, there are forces to publish APIs as late as possible.

In a compromise solution, APIs are published early, but only to a small set of pilot API consumers. Changing the interface is possible, since only the pilot consumers are affected. Pilot API consumers have to expect API changes that will break their clients, but they will also have early access to the API.

Classifying API Evolution

Are all changes to an API equally severe for the clients? In this section we analyze potential changes and classify them according to their severity. We classify changes into three types: backward compatible, forward compatible and incompatible.

Breaking clients are an indicator for severe changes. Thus, the relevant criterion for the severity of a change is this: Would the proposed change of the API break the client?

Backward Compatible Changes

Backward compatibility is given, if an old client can interact with a new API. Despite a change in the API, the API should stay backward compatible with previous implementations. It becomes relevant, when a new API interacts with an old client. Using the new API, the old client should be able to use all the functionality that used to be offered by the old API. Reaching backwards compatibility requires studying old versions of the API. Certain changes to the API are prohibited for backward compatibility, but adding optional elements is usually backward compatible. The following is a list of backward compatible changes:

- Adding query, header or form parameters, as long as they are optional.

- Adding new fields in JSON or XML data structures, as long as they are optional.

- Adding endpoints, e.g. a new REST resource.

- Adding operations to an existing endpoint, e.g. when using SOAP.

- Adding optional fields to the request interfaces.

- Changing mandatory fields to optional fields in an existing API.

Forward Compatible Changes

Forward compatibility is given if a new client can interact with an old API. Despite the change in the client, the API should stay forward compatible with previous implementations.

The new client should be able to use all the functionality of the old API. Forward compatibility is usually much harder to achieve, since it requires anticipating likely future changes. It is usually considered a nice-to-have feature.

Incompatible Changes

If a change to the API breaks the client, the change was incompatible. In general, removing and changing aspects of the API leads to incompatibilities. Here is a non-exhaustive list of incompatible changes:

- Removing or changing data structures, i.e. by changing, removing, or redefining fields in the data structure.

- Removing fields from the request or response (as opposed to making it optional).

- Changing a previously optional request field in the body or parameter into a mandatory field.

- Changing a previously required response field in the body or parameter into an optional field.

- Changing the URI of the API, such as host name, port or path.

- Changing the structure or relationship between request or response fields, e.g. making an existing field a child of some other field.

- Adding a new mandatory field to the data structure.

Reasons for breaking changes can be changed validation rules, new API-products, new database, new infrastructure, or consumers using the API in new ways. If the semantics of the resource changes or the resource has a different (larger, smaller) scope, it is in fact a new resource.

Dealing with Evolution in APIs

When dealing with evolution, one needs to differentiate between compatible and incompatible API changes.

Compatible changes can be implemented with an in-place update. The advantages of in-place updates are that the client does not break and no new version needs to be created.

If possible, incompatible changes should be avoided. If incompatible changes cannot be avoided by anticipating changes, they need to be implemented in such a way that existing clients are not affected. This means that the unchanged API needs to be maintained alongside with the changed API. This results in two versions of the same API.

Hypermedia

When it comes to finding ways to support evolution and longevity, the web itself is a good example. The web has been around for some time and it has scaled massively and has lasted longer than most other software systems. The hypermedia approach of the web has some characteristics that contribute to the longevity of the system. We can use the same principle of the web in other areas as well: Hypermedia means decoupling API implementation from the way clients consume. Clients are smart, follow links and updates and changes of APIs on their own. The creation of new versions for incompatible changes is not necessary. More information on the hypermedia approach is provided in the section on HATEOAS.

Provisioning

If this is for some reason not possible, flexibility has to be introduced in another way. Provisioning is one such approach.

After a change, a bundle of updated configurations is provisioned, by either pushing it to or pulling it from the software. The bundle contains all the information for calling the updated API and to extract the information from the responses.

Only one URI is not allowed to be changed and this is the URI of the provisioning service. The provisioning approach is typically used, when hardware devices call APIs. The provisioning approach might be suitable for many internet of things applications.

Anticipating and Avoiding Evolution

APIs need to be backward compatible. Non-compatible changes to the API, even if they are only small changes, would break the apps that were built with the API. They need to be avoided at all costs. This is why planning ahead with API architecture is extremely important. The API needs to be right the first time it is published. API architecture does not only need to consider, how the API will be used, but also needs to predict, how the API might evolve in the future. But predictions about the future are extremely difficult and often the most innovative uses of the API are not predicted beforehand.

But even if the exact changes cannot be predicted, the fact that there will be changes -- any changes -- can be anticipated. This is why the API needs to be prepared for versioning, right from the start.

If changes to APIs are not absolutely necessary, they should be avoided. Is a new version of the API really necessary? Are the changes really worth the effort of maintaining an additional API? Creating a new version and maintaining this new version alongside the existing API, causes significant overhead and thus, publishing an interface slows down any changes to the API.

Prevent Feature Creep

New API features are constantly required by business and by consumers.

For the API provider, it is easy to give in to these demands and add new functionality to an API portfolio or even to an API. When adding new functionality to an individual API, however, one needs to consider that these features must be supported for the life time of the API.

For APIs, less is more. Less functionality results in simple APIs, and API providers love simple APIs. Thus, APIs and API portfolios need to be simple and need to have a focus. They cannot be everything to everyone. The danger of attempting to provide APIs that suite anyone is feature creep.

Feature creep results in organically grown APIs, whose purpose is hard to understand for new API consumers. It is thus certainly a balancing act to decide about the inclusion of new features in the API and the API portfolio. The API provider needs to be aware of the implications.

API Proxy Architecture

> Simplicity is the ultimate sophistication.
> -- Leonardo DaVinci

In previous chapters we have studied the architecture of the complete API solution, the architecture of the API platform and the design of the API portfolio. In those chapters we have viewed the architecture of each API proxy as a black box, which we have never opened up. In this chapter we open the box to study the architecture of a single API proxy.

Requirements for APIs

Each API solution and each API has an architecture - but not all architectures are equally good. How do we know what a "good" API architecture is? The answer is: it depends -- it depends on the type of the API proxy, and its responsibilities. Based on the responsibilities, we propose a list of desirable properties, which form a benchmark for "good" API proxy architecture.

Armed with these requirements, we can then pick appropriate architectural patterns and architectural styles for building great APIs.

Responsibilities of APIs

APIs typically do not implement any business logic. The business logic and data storage are implemented in the backend systems. So what do APIs typically do? There are four main tasks or responsibilities for any API.

Gathering Data

APIs needs to be able to gather data from various data sources, such as different types of databases, legacy systems or enterprise service buses. For each API it needs to be decided, which backend it should use for gathering data based on the request content or the request context. Sometimes, data from multiple backend systems needs to be requested. Towards the API consumers, the API needs to hide the backend systems used, including their technology stacks, protocols and data formats.

Structuring and Formatting Data

When the data is exposed, it needs to be structured and formatted in such a way that the data can be easily consumed and integrated by the consumer.

For the input and output of the API, the perspective of the API consumer is relevant, not the perspective of the existing backend systems. The API needs to mediate between the nice, clean, simple structure and format presented to the consumer and the complicated format and structure used towards the backend system.

Delivering Data

In general, APIs need to expose easily consumable data in a secure and performant manner. When data is delivered, the consistency of the data needs to be ensured. Appropriate delivery protocols should be used by the API, e.g. for real-time data.

Securing and Protecting

The API enables new business opportunities by opening up the IT systems of the enterprise. This not only leads to new opportunities but also to new security risks. Information could be stolen, or internal systems could be compromised. To deal with these risks, the API needs to ensure that consumers are properly authenticated and authorized to access the data. Moreover, the API not only needs to ensure the security of the exposed data, but also the security and availability of the API platform and - to some extent - the security and availability of the backend systems, which are used by the API. This means that the API needs to protect the API platform and the backend systems from overload and attacks.

Desirable Properties of APIs

Any API needs to fulfill its responsibilities, such as gathering, structuring, delivering and securing data. But this is not enough to make the API really desirable for API consumers.

Which properties does an API need to have to increase its desirability? Desirability can be regarded from the perspective of the consumer or from the perspective of the provider. Ideally, the API exposes properties that satisfy both perspectives.

In the following we list a number of such desirable properties.

Consumer-Centric: The API is made for API consumers, not for the API provider. Regarding the input and output of the API, the perspective of the API consumer is relevant, not the perspective of the existing backend systems. The API needs to mediate between the nice, clean, simple format presented to the consumer and the complicated format used towards the backend system. The value of an API is in removing the complexity for the API consumers, but still be valuable and relevant for the API consumer.

Simple: There should be a low barrier of entry for new API consumers. The API should be simple, so new users can get started quickly and easily. The API should be easy to learn and easy to use. The challenge is to create an API that not only looks much simpler, but actually is much easier to use.

Self-Explanatory, Intuitive and Predictable: The URI needs to be predictable, the parameters need to be self-explanatory and the data objects need to be easy to understand. The API is consistent with the other APIs in the portfolio.

Explorable and Discoverable: An API can be explorable by API consumers. A curious API consumer can explore the API without reading the documentation. APIs should also be discoverable by machines. This requires enough machine readable information in the API and following some conventions.

Well-Documented: Some consumers prefer reading a documentation of the API. For these consumers the API needs to be documented in an easily digestible form, that is fun and exciting, too.

Atomic: The API operates only on one object and does only one thing -- from the API consumer's perspective. The fact that there are several steps involved on the side of the API provider is irrelevant in this context.

Forgiving: The API should deliver error messages that can be understood by the consumer. If the consumer made a mistake, the API provides hints for fixing the mistakes.

Secure and Compliant: The API needs to ensure that it can only be accessed by authenticated and authorized consumers. The API does not leak internal information. The API is compliant with best practices and with security regulations.

Performant, Scalable and Available: For API consumers the performance of the API is an important requirement. A highly performant API allows them to build responsive apps with a great end user experience. Successful APIs become more popular over time. The API and the underlying platform need to be scalable.

Interoperable and Standard-Conform: The API should apply relevant standards and follow industry conventions. Following conventions and standards also improves the understandability of the solution. The APIs should hide any implementation details.

Reusable: The API should not be specific for one API consumer or one project. The API itself should be reusable, but it should also be built from reusable components. This makes APIs consistent. The reusability property is desirable for the API provider, the resulting consistency among the API portfolio is desirable for the API consumer.

Backward Compatible: An API needs to be backward compatible. Old clients need to be supported. If new features do not allow for backward compatibility, a new API or a new API version is created. Once APIs are published and used, they cannot be changed or taken away. Consumers rely on the APIs to work and to work in exactly the described manner. Even though APIs can be very well developed in an agile way, once they are published and used, all the agility has to be left behind and the given version of the API becomes immutable.

How do we use this long list of desirable API properties? We can use it for evaluating the architecture of APIs or we can use it to figure out what we need to improve about the architecture, so it exhibits more desirable properties.

Architectural Patterns

An architectural pattern is a reusable solution to a common challenge in architecture. Several such architectural patterns exist.

From a pragmatic standpoint the question is: How do we know which pattern to use and whether an architectural pattern is appropriate for a specific API? The simple answer is: the resulting API exposes many of the previously stated desirable properties.

For realizing APIs with desirable properties, it is best practice to use the following patterns: the stateless server pattern, the facade pattern and the proxy pattern. In the remainder of this section, we study each of these patterns in detail.

Client Server Patterns

In the client-server architecture, client and server are realized as independent components, running on independent hardware and software stacks. Client and server are loosely coupled and relatively independent. Since client and server are independent but together from a complete application, they need to agree on a mechanism for maintaining the application state.

The state can be for example a set of selections that were made on a previous web site or in a previous API call. In principle, state can be maintained on the server side or on the client side.

In the following we introduce two options: a stateful server and a stateless server. A stateless server pattern is chosen for APIs. To show its properties, we contrast it in the following with a stateful server.

Stateful Server Pattern

When communicating with a stateful server, the client can assume that the state and context of the previous communication is available on the server. The server maintains all the state information in a persistent state object, or a session object, which is preserved in between calls. An identifier for the session is sent to the client. This identifier is called session ID and is used to correlate the state in between calls. The session ID needs to be included in all subsequent calls of the client. Including the session ID into the call ensures that the corresponding session data can be identified on the server.

Stateless Server Pattern

A stateless server does not maintain any information. State can still be used, but it is realized in a different way: the client maintains the application state. The server needs to receive all the necessary information from the client with each API call and it needs to return the updated information in the API response. The server thus ensures, that the client has all necessary information to maintain state. The client keeps the state until the next call to the server.

An advantage of this pattern is the scalability, availability and performance of the solution. The capacity of the solution can be increased by adding new nodes for processing and setting up the load balancer. No server state needs to be migrated to the new nodes. For the same reason, it is equally little effort to scale the solution down by removing processing nodes.

Another advantage is the conceptual simplicity from the API consumers' perspective. No preconditions need to be fulfilled before the API call can be made.

A disadvantage of stateless communication with this client-side form of state-maintenance is the increased network traffic and processing overhead. The data that would be in the session object in a stateful architecture, is serialized and transferred to the client as part of the response, the client deserializes and processes this information and includes the relevant information into the follow-up request. The server receives and processes the data.

Facade Pattern

The responsibility of the API is to expose easily consumable data in a secure and performant manner. Typically, the API does not need to implement the business logic or storage of the exposed data. The API is merely a facade. The business logic is executed behind the facade in internal backend systems, which are hidden from the API consumers.

The API facade uses the principle of information hiding. Hidden behind the facade are complicated backend requests with large and complicated data structures and with meta data that is irrelevant for the consumer. Examples for such hidden backend systems are databases, SOAP services, ESBs, legacy systems, legacy or proprietary protocols, monolithic mainframes or big applications. The facade is used to selectively expose internal systems and make them accessible and consumable by app developers.

A facade consists of an interface and an implementation. To create a facade, two things need to be done:

- Design the interface that would be perfect for your consumers, based on your consumers' needs.

- Create an implementation to mediate between the interface and the backend system. The implementation enforces security, authorizes consumers, monitors usage, and shapes the traffic.

Almost all APIs apply the facade pattern, especially when APIs are used to provide access to legacy systems. An exception may be APIs without any dependencies to legacy systems. They can be found in startups and young companies. In these cases, the API does not require the facade pattern, since the business logic is implemented as part of the API.

Proxy Pattern

A proxy provides an interface to an original object, that is not intended to be exposed directly. Any calls to the proxy are forwarded to the original object. The proxy does not contain any business logic, but functions as a wrapper. The wrapper enriches the functionality of the original object without changing the original object directly.

APIs are typically realized as proxies to the backend systems that deliver the data. APIs provide typical proxy functionality, such as simplifying, transforming, securing and validating requests and responses. The terms API and API proxy are used interchangeably.

An API proxy may contain a single resouce, or it may contain a collection of resources with a shared base path (i.e. the part of the resource's URIs, which is shared by all resources of the API).

Architectural Styles

In general, an architectural style is a large-scale, predefined solution structure. Using an architectural styles helps us to build the system quicker than building everything from scratch. Architectural styles are similar to patterns, but provide a solution for a larger challenge and are thus more generic.

In this section we study several architectural styles for communication in distributed systems. The REST style (Representational State Transfer), the HATEOAS style (Hypermedia As The Engine Of Application State), the RPC style (Remote Procedure Call) and the SOAP style. We compare the approaches, show advantages and disadvantages, commonalities and differences.

APIs can basically be realized using any of these styles. How do we know, whether a particular architectural style is appropriate for a given API? The resulting API exposes many of the previously stated desirable properties.

Most commonly, APIs are realized using REST over HTTP. This is why one can assume in practice that APIs are realized with the REST style.

REST Style

REST (Representational State Transfer) is an architectural style for services, and as such it defines a set of architectural constraints and agreements. A service, which complies with the REST constraints, is said to be RESTful.

REST is designed to make optimal use of an HTTP-based infrastructure and due to the success of the web, HTTP-based infrastructure, such as servers, caches and proxies, are widely available. The web, which is based on HTTP, provides some proof for an architecture that not only scales extremely well but also has longevity. The basic idea of REST is to transfer the ideas that worked well for the web and apply them to web services.

But before we get started with explaining the basic ideas of REST, let me clear some common misconceptions about REST: REST is not a standard. REST is not a protocol either. REST is an architectural style, which is typically used in combination with the HTTP protocol.

REST Concepts

The central concept in REST is the concept of a resource. A resource is a data structure, which can be serialized to various concrete representations, such as a JSON representation or an XML representation. REST APIs expose and manipulate these resources. An API (proxy) typically exposes one or several resources.

Resources are almost like objects in the object oriented programming paradigm. This comparison holds, as far as it concerns the presence of data fields, values and methods, which manipulate the data fields. One of the important differences, however, is that in REST, the methods are restricted to the set of HTTP methods (sometimes they are also called HTTP verbs). This set of allowed methods is called uniform resource interface. Besides the HTTP methods specified in the uniform resource interface, no other methods can be used to manipulate the resource. No other methods can be stated in API requests, neither in the HTTP body nor in the base path nor in the parameters.

REST APIs mostly perform CRUD (create, read, update, delete) operations, which can be easily mapped to HTTP methods. Creation can be performed by a POST or PUT, reading is performed by GET, updating is performed by PUT and a deletion is performed by a DELETE. Each of the HTTP methods has a specific purpose and also a specific set of characteristics. Relevant characteristics of HTTP methods are safety and idempotency. Idempotent methods may be executed repeatedly without altering the end result; executing the method multiple times has the same effect as executing the method only once. Safe methods do not have any side effects, do not change the state of the resource and are read-only.

REST is incompatible with the commonly used procedure-oriented style for web services, where procedures are first class objects. When defining procedure-oriented interfaces, activities or operations are the abstraction and services encapsulate procedures. With resource-oriented interfaces, data structures are the abstractions, and a resource model is the service interface. When building resource-oriented systems, a few fixed operations are used to operate on resource interfaces.

REST Constraints

REST defines a number of constraints for API design. Many of the REST constraints are actually HTTP constraints, and REST leverages these HTTP constraints for web services.

The REST style ensures that APIs use HTTP correctly. By using HTTP correctly in APIs, you get many desirable properties "for free". These constraints limit the freedom of design, not every design is allowed any more. REST imposes the following constraints:

- Use of HTTP capabilities as far as possible.

- Design of resources (nouns), not methods or operations (verbs).

- Use of the uniform interface, defined by HTTP methods, which have well-specified semantics.

- Stateless communication between client and server.

- Use of loose coupling and independence of the requests.

- Use of HTTP return codes.

- Use of media types.

Advantages of REST

Each of these constraints contributes to the desirable system properties. In return for following these constraints, designers can expect systems that have several desirable properties.

An advantage of REST is the scalability of the system. Since REST systems are stateless and the requests are independent, it is easier to scale the system by adding another server. The same features also allow for fault tolerance, and an improved availability and reliability of the complete system.

Another advantage of using this architectural style is the performance of the resulting solutions. Caching functionality can be achieved for free, i.e. without any additional implementations, since it is already taken care of by the HTTP infrastructure. By using REST it is ensured that APIs can use existing caching mechanisms.

Another advantage is the support for handling multiple content types. An API may be able to deliver the resource in multiple, alternative formats, and the client may be able to read responses in only one of these formats. The content type negotiation mechanisms defines how client API can exchange information about their capabilities and negotiate the appropriate content type. This mechanism is inherited from HTTP.

Another advantage of REST is its simplicity. The creation of a new REST API does not require a lot of overhead. In comparison, the creation of SOAP services requires a larger overhead, due to the specification of WSDL files with a compatible implementation.

The REST limitation to the uniform resource interface contributes to the explorability and discoverability of APIs. With some experience in HTTP, the available methods are self-explanatory, intuitive and predictable, since the same methods are used in each and every API. As a result, consumers can quickly access the service and perform calls.

REST services provide visibility, since it makes the intent of a request available and accessible to any HTTP component. Roy Fielding defines visibility as the "ability of a component to monitor or mediate the interaction between two other components". HTTP ensures -- when used correctly -- visibility. The correct use of HTTP in APIs requires the correct HTTP methods and appropriate status codes.

HATEOAS Style

HATEOAS is an abbreviation for Hypermedia As The Engine Of Application State. HATEOAS is an extension of REST and any of the constraints and advantages of REST also apply to HATEOAS. HATEOAS has additional constraints, allowing for more dynamic architectures. These constraints allow clients to explore any API without any a-priori knowledge of data formats or of the API itself.

HATEOAS Concepts

According to HATEOAS, APIs are self-descriptive. All actions, which can be performed on resources are described in the representations of the resources in the form of annotated links. Each resource contains links to other resources.

The annotated links can be navigated by a generic client, which can interpret and follow links. Since all resources are linked, the client only need to have access to the root resource. From there on, the client can follow the links to reach any other resource. This might be used to define a very dynamic architecture. Since the client always navigates to the needed resource by following links, it is easy to provide updates and make changes in this architecture. There are no breaking changes, because the client does not make any assumption about the API. All meta-information is obtained right before the call. If the API is changed, the additional resources, which link to the changed resource need to be updated, with new links and new associated meta-information.

The semantics of the resources is provided by media types. This is why the HATEOAS style is also known as the hypermedia style.

An API following the HATEOAS style can be modeled as a state machine, consisting of states and transitions. Resources correspond to the states and the links between the resources correspond to the transitions of the state machine. A client works with this state machine by extracting links and following them.

HATEOAS Constraints

- All REST principles apply.

- Resources are linked to each other. Representations of API responses contain hyperlinks pointing to other resources.

- The semantics of API responses is provided by the media types.

Advantages of HATEOAS

- Flexibility: new versions, or changed media types can be realized without breaking any clients. For example, it is in the hands of the server to transparently change the URI structure.

- Simple client logic: the client does not need any a-priori knowledge of the API.

- Simple evolution of APIs: API and client do not need to evolve in synch, as they need to with REST, RPC or SOAP.

RPC Style

RPC is an abbreviation for Remote Procedure Call. RPC is an architectural style for distributed systems. It has been around since the 1980s. Today the most widely used RPC styles are JSON-RPC and XML-RPC. Even SOAP can be considered to follow an RPC architectural style.

The central concept in RPC is the procedure. The procedures do not need to run on the local machine, but they can run on a remote machine within the distributed system. When using an RPC framework, calling a remote procedure should be as simple as calling a local procedure.

How does RPC work?

A remote procedure is invoked from a client by serializing the client's parameters and additional information into a message and sending the message to a server. The server receives the message, deserializes its content, performs the requested calculation and sends a result back to the client, using the same serialization/deserialization mechanism.

JSON-RPC

JSON-RPC is used to call a single procedure on a remote machine. When serializing the request or response it uses a well-defined JSON schema for JSON-RPC.

It not only defines a JSON schema for the serialization of requests and responses into JSON, but also defines the fault handling with error messages. It is currently specified in version 2 [19].

XML-RPC

XML-RPC is used to call a single procedure on a remote machine.

As its name suggests, it uses XML for serializing the procedure request (methodCall) and response (methodResponse). Additionally, messages for fault handling are described. The nesting of XML allows transporting complex data structures. XML-RPC has been around since 1998 [20] and later evolved into SOAP.

SOAP Style

SOAP follows the RPC style and exposes procedures as central concepts (e.g. getCustomer). It is standardized by the W3C [21] and is the most widely used protocol for web services. SOAP style architectures are in widespread use, however, typically only for company internal use or for services called by trusted partners.

SOAP offers bindings to a variety of transport protocols, such as HTTP, SMTP, TCP, UDP or JMS. SOAP is based on XML and actually evolved from XML-RPC. A serialized SOAP message is wrapped by an envelope containing a header with meta information, and a body with a request, a response or a fault. Complex data structures for request and response can be defined and described by XML schema. The interface of SOAP services is described by a dedicated, standardized language, the Web Service Description Language WSDL [16].

SOAP offers many extensions, for example for transferring binary data, for security, federation, trust, encryption and signing - just to name a few. These extensions are also known as WS-*. Some of the extensions are standardized, while others are product-specific.

Architectural Trade-offs

APIs can be realized using any of the presented architectural styles (REST, HATEOAS, RPC or SOAP).

Sometimes there are trade-offs with other architectural demands. Good judgement has to be used to determine which demand wins. Examples of such competing architectural demands:

- Information abstraction
- Simplicity
- Loose coupling

- Network efficiency

- Resource granularity

- Convenience for the consumer

In the following we compare some of the most common alternatives for API styles.

RPC in Comparison to REST

Not every service that is exposed over HTTP is compliant with the REST constraints. Sometimes one can find services, which are advertised as being RESTful, but in reality they follow the RPC style. In fact, there may even be a grey zone between REST and RPC, when a service implements some features of REST and some of RPC. The Richardson Maturity Model can be used for determining the degree to which a services is RESTful. The following levels are defined:

- Level 0: Services use an RPC style.

- Level 1: Services expose resources. Larger services are broken down into resources.

- Level 2: Services use HTTP methods correctly. Services use HTTP infrastructure efficiently.

- Level 3: Hypermedia is used according to HATEOAS. The service is self-documenting and flexible.

According to Roy Fielding, the REST style requires level 3, which is in fact HATEOAS. However, typically people speak about REST services, even if only levels 1 or 2 are reached. REST at lower levels is sometimes called "pragmatic REST".

Here are a couple of simple, practical tricks to determine if a service is not RESTful:

- If the name of the service is a verb instead of a noun, the service is likely RPC and not RESTful.

- If the name of the service to be executed is encoded in the request body, the service is likely RPC and thus not RESTful.

- If the back-button in the web-application does not work as expected, the service is not stateless and thus not RESTful.

- If the service or website does not behave as expected after turning cookies off, the service is not stateless and not RESTful.

HATEOAS in Comparison to REST

HATEOAS is a specialization of REST, so those two contenders have a lot of commonalities. This is why we have to look into the details to compare the two styles. For this purpose we can use the four levels of the Richardson Maturity Model:

- Level 0: Services use an RPC style.

- Level 1: Services expose resources. Larger services are broken down into resources.

- Level 2: Services use HTTP methods correctly. Services use HTTP infrastructure efficiently.

- Level 3: Hypermedia is used according to HATEOAS. The service is self-documenting and flexible.

According to the model, HATEOAS is the most mature version of REST. However, HATEOAS is not widely used in practice for a variety of reasons. Realizing a HATEOAS-based solution requires quite a large paradigm shift for the designers and way more advanced and intelligent API clients than are typically used and built today. This is why HATEOAS mainly serves as a vision for the long term development of RESTful API design.

Pragmatic REST at level 2 is the architectural style, which is most commonly used today. It strikes an attractive balance between familiarity and advantageous non-functional properties. Pragmatic REST is not as foreign to designers as HATEOAS, but still provides many benefits, such as simplicity, cacheability, performance and statelessness.

SOAP in Comparison to REST

SOAP makes data available as services (e.g. getCustomer), REST makes data available as resources (e.g. /customer/123/address).

REST services are considered lightweight, SOAP services are considered heavy weight. This has two reasons. SOAP services are typically coarse-grained, and deliver comprehensive data structures. REST services are typically fine-grained and serve bite-sized data structures. SOAP messages contain a lot of meta data and only support verbose XML structures for requests and responses. Also, due to their large size, SOAP services are considered complicated for service providers and for service consumers. REST services strip their data structures down to the necessary elements.

SOAP can be bound to many protocols, including HTTP, TCP, UDP and SMTP. REST is limited to HTTP. SOAP is usually used over HTTP, however, it is not optimized for HTTP: SOAP uses the HTTP-POST method, is thus non-idempotent and does not offer any cacheability. SOAP services do not offer visibility, since no semantic information about the method can be deduced. REST is optimized for the HTTP protocol and can make full use of its caching and content-negotiation features.

SOAP is well-suited for enterprise integration, due to its rigid structure, and its security and authorization capabilities. SOAP is good for transactions or for enforcing a formal software contract between API and client, based on a legal contract between API provider and API consumer. SOAP is typically used for integration with enterprise partners.

REST is well-suited for APIs that are intended for wide adoption with many API consumers. Due to the relatively simple data structures and fine granularity, REST is well suited for devices with limited computing resources, such as mobile devices and for the internet of things.

API Description Languages

Whenever APIs need to be communicated among various stakeholders, APIs needs to be described in some from. Thus, it should be as easy as possible to describe APIs. Specialized languages can support the crafting of useful API descriptions by providing appropriate abstractions and language concepts. Such specialized languages are API description languages.

In their short history, the role of API description languages has changed significantly. The original purpose of API description languages was the creation of API documentation, in a similar way as JavaDoc provides a language for documenting Java programs. Today, API description languages can be used for many additional purposes during the design and development process of APIs, not only for their original purpose of generating a pretty documentation.

API description languages are machine readable specifications of the API. Machine readable specifications can be used for automating tasks in API development. If used correctly, automation has the potential to increase the productivity of API development.

We will see more examples for increasing the efficiency of API development later. Here is just a small example as an appetizer:

The API description can be used for the automated generation of the API implementation. Think about it as a compiler that takes an API desciption as input and produces the API implementation as output. This functionality supports the work of the API provider. But this is not all: The same API description can also be used by the API consumer for generating the implementation of client-stub-code for the app consuming the API. This functionality supports the consumer. Both cases are based on the same API description.

In this chapter we introduce the most important tools for API design: API description languages. If used correctly, API description languages are very powerful tools that can be far more than just languages. They can serve as the "single source of truth" and as the main reference for all aspects of API design and development. They can also be used to automate many tasks in the software development process of APIs.

What are API Description Languages?

API description languages are domain specific languages, which are especially suited for describing APIs. They are both human readable and machine readable languages, much like programming languages. They are intuitive languages that can be easily written, read and understood by API developers and API designers alike. API description languages are also precise, leave little room for ambiguity and are very expressive and powerful. They have a well-defined syntax, which makes it possible to process them automatically by software.

106

Compared to programming languages or API implementation languages, API description languages use a higher level of abstraction and a declarative paradigm. This means that they can be used to express the "what" instead of the "how". For example, they define the data structure of the possible responses (the "what"), instead of describing how the response is computed (the "how"). This makes them very well suited for expressing the architecture of each API proxy in the portfolio and the design of the API portfolio as a whole.

API Description Language vs. API Development Language

An API platform should provide two types of languages. The first language should be a higher-level language, which can be used for designing APIs and for expressing the "what". It is called API description language. The second language that should be provided by an API platform is a lower-level language, which is used for implementing APIs and for expressing the "how". This is the API development language.

An API description languages is a domain specific language for expressing API design. API platforms provide not only the language, but also design tools for creating API interface designs, tools for generating documentation, tests and the implementation based on API descriptions.

An API development language is a special purpose language that is used for implementing APIs. It incorporates many API building blocks as language constructs. The language offers a way for combining the building blocks into meaningful APIs.

What is the relation between API description languages and API development languages? First, APIs should be designed using an API description language. Some API platforms have support for API description languages built in. This means that the platform supports the parsers and code generators for a specific API description language. The generated implementations should be expressed in the API development language.

Usage

In this section we present several use cases for API descriptions. These use cases are not chosen for their completeness, but they are chosen to convey the central role of API descriptions for the design and development of APIs. API descriptions are central, since they can support all phases of API design and development.

Communication and Documentation

Since an API is an interface connecting two or more software systems, it is important that the API is understood by the involved developers on all sides. Some of the involved developers are on the side of the API provider and busy developing the API. Other developers are on the consumer side. They typically develop apps that use the API. The idea of loose coupling of services is great, as long as it is ensured that the services are well understood by the developers on API provider side and on API consumer side.

To provide a shared understanding of an API, the API needs to be well documented. This is all the more important as the developers are not co-located and can quickly share their insights. Instead, they are spread out over different companies, countries, continents and time zones. An appropriate documentation can help in this case. This is why the documentation of APIs is extremely important for both developers of the server-side API implementation and for the client-side API consumers.

Documentation is usually delivered as written prose in a document. Alternatively, some developers might consider the code sufficient as a form of documentation. A short and precise description of all the important design decisions for the API has advantages to prose documentation and to code as documentation. Code is precise but is too long, too complicated to understand, and may not be publishable due to intellectual property or security considerations. Prose documentation may simply be not precise enough.

The original purpose of API description languages is providing human readable API documentation. To relieve the developer from the burden of formatting pretty HTML pages, domain specific languages (DSL) for documenting APIs have been created. Based on such a DSL, the documentation of the API can be automatically generated. If you have used Java, you might be familiar with JavaDoc, an approach for generating documentation from specially marked annotations in Java programs. A similar approach is taken here; the documentation is generated based on a special purpose language: the API description language.

If the API documentation is written in an API description language, it has some attractive properties. The API documentation contains only relevant information and this information is available in a structured, ordered and compact form. This makes API description languages suitable for being written by developers.

109

The reason is that writing an API description is actually very similar to writing a program. No formatting or styling needs to be provided, but the documentation needs to follow rigid syntactic rules. In this respect, API description languages are similar to programming languages. API descriptions written in these languages are thus ideally suited for machine processing. Parsers can take the description apart and build an abstract syntax tree. This abstract syntax tree is then traversed by generators to produce other representations, for example a pretty HTML page.

While the API developer might enjoy the simplicity and clarity of the API description, the API consumer might expect the API documentation to be a pretty, colorful and interactive HTML page. To allow for both views of API provider and API consumer, a generator is used to extract the information from the API description and to generate the corresponding human-readable documentation.

API descriptions also enable the creation of an interactive documentation. Interactive documentation is not only meant to be read like regular documentation, it also includes a testing bed for the APIs. API consumers can make test calls to the real API or to a simulation of the API directly from the documentation page. They do not even have to use any external tools.

API consumers typically have a choice between alternative APIs, which roughly do the same thing. The first point of contact between API consumer and API is the documentation. A documentation, which is better than the alternatives and ideally is interactive, it may convince an API consumer to shortlist this API.

Design Repository

The API description of an API proxy is the central reference of truth for this API.

If you are ever in doubt, which version of the API accepts a certain parameter or which status codes are returned by the API, the API description is the definitive, authoritative point of reference.

The API description contains all the important design decisions for that API proxy. Not only a single API proxy should be documented, but the complete API portfolio, including the API descriptions of all API proxies. To provide a history and synchronized access in a distributed development team, the API descriptions should be put under version control, e.g. in a GIT or SVN repository.

Contract Negotiation

From a process perspective the API description can serve as a design contract. This contract can be used for agreements between API designer and API developer or as a contract between API consumer and API provider.

The API description enables contract-first design. Both contracting parties negotiate this contract, decide on it and rely on this contract during the implementation and maintenance phases.

Traditionally, app developers would need to wait for the API to be finished. Contract first design allows starting the implementation of the app by the consumer before the provider has finished building the API. Thus contract first design allows for a very efficient development process with a much quicker turn around time. It allows app developers to bring their apps to market quicker than before. In contract-first design, the precise description of the design contract is essential. This is the strength of API description languages.

API Implementation

Since the API description is machine readable, it can be used for automating tasks in software development.

Such an approach follows the ideas of generative software development, model driven development and domain specific languages. If used correctly, these approaches have the potential to increase the productivity of software development.

The API description can be used by the API provider to automatically generate API skeletons. An API skeleton contains some important pieces of the implementation, it is, however, not complete. The skeleton needs to be extended and filled with manual implementation before the API can be used.

These skeletons may contribute to a higher speed for API implementation as well as to a higher quality of the API implementation. The speed may be higher, because the developer does not need to write all the code himself, but a large portion of the code is already written for him automatically. The quality of the API may be improved by code generation, since the generated code is consistent with the API description.

When the first iteration of the API implementation is generated from the API description, the API implementation is created from scratch. There is no prior implementation to take care of and the API implementation initially only consists of the API skeleton.

A challenge for automated code generation are updates to the API description. If a previous implementation already exists, the newly generated code needs to be merged with the existing code. Depending on the code generation framework, this might be supported by specific code markers, which are used to separate the generated code skeleton from the API implementation.

Client Implementation

On the API consumer side, the API description can be used for generating client stubs for accessing the API. With an appropriate code generator, the client stub can be generated for the programming language used by the consumer.

For the API consumer, code generation has a couple of advantages. By generating the client stub for accessing the API, it is ensured that the implementation actually matches the specified contract. For the API consumer, code generation speeds up the development process.

Support during client implementation is only possible, if the API provider makes the API description available to the consumers. The API description of the API should be served by a specific endpoint of the API.

Discovery

How does the client know about the capabilities of the API? One answer is: the client does not need to know, since the API needs to be understood by the API consumer and he develops the client. The consumer can learn about the API from the human-readable documentation. Another answer is: the client needs to be able to explore or discover the capabilities of the API programmatically. With such an automated discovery mechanism, an app may include new APIs, which have not been known at design time.

To enable such an implementation, an API description of the API portfolio should be served by a specific endpoint. This allows the caller to discover each API within the portfolio by downloading and parsing the API description. A precondition is that the API provider made the API description available to the consumers.

Simulation

A simulation can provide a first impression of the finished API to the consumer. In the early phases of API design, a simulation can be presented to pilot consumers for eliciting their initial feedback. The pilot consumers can even base first demos of their apps on the API simulation.

In general, a model of the real world is needed to create a simulation. An API description contains such a model. The model is provided in the form of the interface specifications that are necessary to build a simple simulation or mockup.

A specification of the input data in the form of query parameters, form parameters, header parameters path parameters or a data structure in the message body is included in an API description. The simulation can verify input according to the specification.

A specification of the error messages is included in an API description. The simulation can produce error behavior according to the specification.

An example response is specified, which can be served by the simulated API. Sometimes an example is directly provided as part of the description, sometimes the example has to be constructed based on a generic specification of the data structure.

Language Features

The API description is a technical contract between API provider and API consumer, so it is important that the designed contract is unambiguous and clear.

A contract should provide clarity to all involved stakeholders and should enable simultaneous development of both the consuming and providing software components. This is why the language for expressing the contract -- the API description language -- needs to have the following features:

- Compactness: The contract should be as compact as possible, reduced to the necessary and the relevant. Repetitions should be avoided by proper language abstractions.

- Precision: Since the API description language is used for specifying a contract, it needs to be precise and unambiguous.

- Relevance: The language constructs need to be relevant for API design and should not contain unnecessary or superfluous information.

- Support for agility: The API description language should support an agile and iterative development approach. Based on a first iteration or a rough draft of an API design, it should be possible to create a refined second iteration. The level of detail can be added or removed.

- Clarity and structure: An API description language should have a well-defined syntax, thus providing clarity and structure. In contrast, a prose description of the API tends to be unclear and ambiguous.

- Support for communication: You do not need to be a programmer to understand an API description. Architects or business should be able to use an API description as well. The generated HTML documentation is available to an even larger audience.

- Support for quick validation: It should be possible to validate an API description quickly and easily, possibly in an automated fashion.

- Intuitive: It should be possible to use the API description language without a lot of training.

Any API description language should have the properties listed above. Today, a number of API description languages are available. Which should be chosen? The most popular and widespread API description languages are Swagger, RAML, Blueprint, Mashery I/O Docs, WADL and WSDL.

WADL [17] and WSDL [16] have been around for a long time, their use is widespread, they can be used for API design, however, they have not been created specifically for RESTful API design and thus lack important features. The Web Application Description Language (WADL) was created for web applications. It does not contain any built-in support for JSON schema, or commonly used security schemes such as OAuth. The Web Service Description Language (WSDL) is used for describing SOAP services. It supports RPC-style services, which exchange XML-based SOAP requests and responses. WSDL cannot be used for describing REST services, since it does neither support JSON data structures, nor API security schemes such as OAuth.

The languages Swagger [12], RAML [13], API Blueprint [15] and Mashery I/O Docs [16] have been created specifically for RESTful API design. In the following we introduce Swagger and RAML, two popular languages for creating API descriptions.

Swagger

Swagger is a popular API description language. Excellent tool support is available and Swagger is supported by many API platforms, such as Apigee, 3scale, WSO2 and Dell Boomi.

Introduction

This description is based on Swagger v2.0 [12]. It is not a replacement for a complete and thorough introduction to Swagger. This section intends to provide some intuition for the usage of Swagger.

There are actually two variants of Swagger 2.0, one variant has a JSON syntax and the other variant has a YAML syntax. Only the YAML [29] syntax is presented here. The basic syntax of YAML applies, which uses whitespace for structuring. A YAML file is hierarchically structured and consists of properties, which are realized as key-value pairs and objects. Objects have child properties, which are indented with whitespace. It is possible to have lists as values, they are presented in squared brackets []. There can also be lists of properties, in this case a minus - is used in front of each property in the list.

An API description in Swagger contains the following main information items:

- Basic information and meta-information, such as name, title, and location of the API and user documentation. This information is captured in the root element.

- A list of resources including methods, schemas and parameters

117

- Reusable elements such as data definitions, responses, parameters and securityDefinitions

Example

Let's get started by looking at the API portfolio of an online book store. This API portfolio contains two APIs, one collection API delivering a listing of all the books and a book API, providing details for a specific book, which is identified by an ISBN. In the following we describe this API portfolio using Swagger.

```
swagger: '2.0'
info:
  title: Book API
  description: The book API ...
  version: v1
host: domain.com
schemes:
  - https
basePath: /v1
produces:
  - application/json
paths:
  /books:
    get:
      summary: Book listings
      description: Provides a list of all available
                  books written in a specific language
      parameters:
        - $ref: '#/parameters/languageSelection'
      responses:
        200:
          description: A listing of the books
          schema:
            type: array
            items:
              $ref: '#/definitions/Book'
  /books/{isbn}:
    get:
      summary: Book information
      description: Information about the book
```

```yaml
      parameters:
        - name: isbn
          in: path
          description: ISBN of the book to get
          required: true
          type: string
      responses:
        200:
          description: The book with the given ISBN
          schema:
            $ref: '#/definitions/Book'
      security:
        - oauthImplicit: [read_books]
parameters:
  languageSelection:
    name: lang
    in: query
    description: select the language of the books
    type: string
definitions:
  Book:
    properties:
      title:
        type: string
      author:
        type: string
      price:
        type: string
      isbn:
        type: string
      language:
        type: string
      description:
        type: string
    example:
      title: Walden,
      author: Henry David Thoreau,
      price: 8.90,
      isbn: 123456789X,
      language: en,
      description: A reflection on simple living in
nature
securityDefinitions:
  basicAuth:
    type: basic
  apiKeyAuth:
    type: apiKey
```

```
      name: api_key
      in: header
  oauthImplicit:
    type: oauth2
    authorizationUrl:
      https://domain.com/oauth/authorization
    flow: implicit
    scopes:
      write_books: modify books
      read_books: read books
```

As you can see in the example, Swagger is a hierarchically structured language. Sub elements are indented relative to their parent elements.

All elements of this example are taken apart and explained in the following subsections.

Root Element

The root element is at the top of the Swagger description. It is used to describe basic information about the API and to provide some meta information. The root element includes the following properties:

- `host:` The property host specifies the host name or IP address of the host, on which a running instance of the API or an API simulation are or will be deployed.

- `basePath:` The basePath is the part of the URI of the API, which follows directly after the host name. It points to a running instance of the API or of an API simulation.

- `schemes:` The schemes in the root element are the default protocols used for this API. The scheme property can have the values `ws, wss, http, https`. This default configuration can be overwritten for each method.

120

- `consumes:` The consumes property defines the media types consumed by the APIs.

- `produces:` The produces property defines the media types produced by the APIs.

- `info:` The property info specifies meta information about all the APIs in the portfolio. It includes fields such as:

  - `title:` Title of the API portfolio.

  - `description:` Description of the API portfolio.

  - `termsOfService:` Link to a terms of service description for the API portfolio.

  - `contact:` Contact information, including name, email, URI.

  - `license:` Link to the license of the API portfolio.

  - `version:` Version of the API portfolio.

- `paths:` The path property defines the resources of the API. We will study this element closer in the section on resources.

- `responses:` Reusable definitions of responses. We will study this element closer in the section on resources.

- `parameters:` Reusable definitions of parameters. We will study this element closer in the section on parameters and in the section on reusable elements.

- `definitions:` Reusable definitions of data structures. We will study this element closer in the section on reusable elements.

- **securityDefinitions:** Reusable definitions of security schemes. We will study this element closer in the section on security.

- **security:** Default security for this API, references one of the securityDefinitions. We will study this element closer in the section on security.

Resources

Resources are described in the `paths` property. Each resource is identified by its relative path (relative to the basePath). For each resource, a number of HTTP methods (GET, POST, PUT, DELETE, etc.) can be listed.

Methods

For each method, the following properties can be defined:

- **summary:** One line summary describing the purpose of the resource.

- **description:** Verbose description of the resource.

- **schemes:** The schemes of this particular method. The scheme property can have the values `ws, wss, http, https`.

- **security:** The security mechanism, which is used to protect this API.

- **parameters:** List of input parameters, which can be provided for this API. Different types of input parameters (query parameter, header parameter, form parameter or path parameter) are supported. These parameter types are described in more detail later in this chapter.

- `responses:` List of response types, which can be expected from this API. The response types are identified by their status code. Responses are described in more detail later in this chapter.

- `consumes:` The media types consumed by the resource.

- `produces:` The media types produced by the resource.

- `operationId:` Unique name of this resource.

An example of a resource with a GET method:

```
swagger: '2.0'
paths:
  /books:
    get:
      summary: Book listings
      description: The book listings based on a title
      schemes: https
      security:
        oauthImplicit
          - read_books
      parameters:
        ...
      responses:
        ...
      produces: application/json
```

Responses

Each method of a resource offers a list of possible responses. Responses are identified by the HTTP status code they provide. A response has the following properties:

- `description:` Description of the response.

- **schema:** Definition of the HTTP body of the response. It can be a primitive type (string, number, integer, boolean, file), an array or an object.

- **headers:** Header parameters of the response. It is structured in a similar way as the header parameters of the request.

- **examples:** An example response.

```
swagger: '2.0'
paths:
  /books/{isbn}:
    get:
      summary: Book listings
      responses:
        200:
          description: Successful response
                       with a book listing
          schema:
            $ref: '#/definitions/Book'
          examples:
            application/json:
              title: Walden
              author: Henry David Thoreau
              price: 8.90
              description: A reflection on simple
                           living in nature
              isbn: 123456789X
```

Schema

Swagger differentiates schema definitions and schema references. Schema references merely refer to a previously defined schema. Schema definitions are used to define a data structure. They are properties of the root element. They are based on the abstract syntax of JSON Schema [25]. If Swagger is used in the YAML variant, the schema definition can be expressed in the concrete syntax of YAML, as shown in the following snippet.

Besides the specification of the data structure, a schema definition may also include an example instance of the data structure.

```
swagger: '2.0'
definitions:
  Book:
    properties:
      title:
        type: string
      author:
        type: string
      price:
        type: string
      isbn:
        type: string
      language:
        type: string
      description:
        type: string
    example:
      title: Walden,
      author: Henry David Thoreau,
      price: 8.90,
      isbn: 123456789X,
      language: en,
      description: A    reflection    on    simple    living
                   in nature
  ErrorModel:
    type: object
    required:
      - message
      - code
    properties:
```

```
    message:
      type: string
    code:
      type: integer
      minimum: 100
      maximum: 600
  ExtendedErrorModel:
    allOf:
      - $ref: '#/definitions/ErrorModel'
      - type: object
        required:
          - rootCause
        properties:
          rootCause:
            type: string
```

The data definitions can describe JSON or XML data structures depending on the mime type declared in the surrounding element of the schema reference. For XML data structures, additional information about the mapping to XML schema can be provided in the xml property. It contains child properties such as a name replacements, declaration of the namespace, declaration of the prefix, or by the keyword attribute an indication is provided if a property should be translated into an attribute or an element.

Parameters

Several types of parameters are supported. All parameters have the following properties:

- name: Name of the parameter

- type: Data type of the parameter. It can be string, number, integer, boolean, file, array

- `in:` Type of the parameter. Can be `path`, `query`, `formData`, `header`, or `body`. Interestingly, the body is listed as an input parameter.

- `schema:` Schema of the HTTP body of the request. It is only available if the property in is set to `body`. The `schema` is usually not defined in place, but it is referenced, e.g. `$ref: '#/definitions/User'`.

- `required:` Indicates if the parameter is optional or required. Can be `true` or `false`.

- `description:` A verbose description of the parameter.

- `format:` Additional formatting rules for the parameter values.

- `items:` Describes the elements in an array. It is only available if `type` is set to `array`.

- `collectionFormat:` Format for serializing an array. Possible values are: `csv`, `ssv`, `tsv`, `pipes`, or `multi`. The default value is `csv`.

```
swagger: '2.0'
paths:
  /books/{isbn}:
    get:
      summary: Book information
      parameters:
        - name: isbn
          in: path
          description: ISBN of the book to get
          required: true
          type: string
      responses:
        ...
```

Path parameters are described by `in:path`. For path parameters a placeholder is defined in the path of the resource. The name of the placeholder is the name of the parameter.

Query parameters are described by `in:query`. Form parameters are described by `in:form`. Header parameters are described by `in:header`. Input parameters, which are provided in the HTTP body, are described by `in:body`.

Reusable Elements

When describing a complete API portfolio containing several APIs, API descriptions would be quite repetitive. This is actually a good sign, since it shows that API governance was applied on the API portfolio to ensure consistency. Elements which are consistently applied throughout the description of the API portfolio, can be factored out into reusable elements.

Some elements of a Swagger description can be reused by declaring them once in the root element and referencing them later. The reusable elements can be `parameters`, `schemas` and `responses`. References to reusable elements are realized by the reference object. It has the following format.

```
$ref: '#/definitions/Book'
```

Reusable parameters can be declared in the `parameters` property of the root element.

```
swagger: '2.0'
parameters:
  skipParam:
    name: skip
    in: query
    description: number of items to skip
    required: true
    type: integer
    format: int32
```

Reusable schemas can be declared in the `definitions` property of the root element.

```
swagger: '2.0'
definitions:
  Book:
    properties:
      isbn:
        type: string
      title:
        type: string
```

Reusable responses can be declared in the `responses` property of the root element.

```
swagger: '2.0'
responses:
  NotFound:
    description: Entity not found.
  IllegalInput:
    description: Illegal input for operation.
  GeneralError:
    description: General Error
    schema:
      $ref: '#/definitions/GeneralError'
```

Security

Swagger differentiates the abstract definition of the security schemes and the binding of the security schemes to a particular API.

Security Definition

A list of security schemes is abstractly defined in the property `securityDefinitions`. Each item in the list has a name and the following properties:

- `type:` Type of the security scheme. Can have the values basic, apiKey or oauth2

- `description:` Description of the security scheme.

- `name:` Name of the header or query parameter, which contains the apiKey. Only relevant for `type: apiKey`.

- `in:` Indicates if the apiKey is transmitted as header or query parameter. Can have the values `query` or `header`. Only relevant for `type: apiKey`.

- `flow:` Indicates the OAuth grant type and can have the values `implicit` (for implicit grant), `password` (for resource owner password credential grant), `application` (for client credential grant) or `accessCode` (for authorization code grant). Only relevant for `type: oauth2`.

- `authorizationUrl:` URI of the OAuth authorization endpoint. Only relevant for `type: oauth2`.

- `tokenUrl:` URI of the OAuth token endpoint. Only relevant for `type: oauth2`.

- `scopes:` Available OAuth scopes. Maps the name of the scope to a short description of the scope's meaning. Only relevant for `type: oauth2`.

An example for a security definition:

```
swagger: '2.0'
securityDefinitions:
  basicAuth:
    type: basic
  apiKeyAuth:
    type: apiKey
    name: api_key
    in: header
  oauthImplicit:
    type: oauth2
    authorizationUrl:
https://domain.com/oauth/authorization
    flow: implicit
    scopes:
      write_books: modify book listings
      read_books: read book listings
```

Security Binding

Each operation can use its own security scheme, by referencing to one of the declared security definitions. For OAuth security schemes, a list of the required scopes is provided.

Example for API keys:

```
swagger: '2.0'
paths:
  /books:
    get:
      summary: Book listings
      security:
        apiKeyAuth: [ ]
```

Example for OAuth:

```
swagger: '2.0'
paths:
  /books/{isbn}:
    get:
      summary: Book information
      security:
        oauthImplicit:
```

```
- read_books
```

RAML

RAML [13] is an API description language, which was invented by Mulesoft. Spelled out, RAML stands for the RESTful API Modeling Language. In addition to the language, a set of RAML tools are offered for describing, producing, consuming, and visualizing RESTful APIs. RAML is supported by some API platforms, such as Mulesoft Anypoint, 3scale and Restlet.

Introduction

This description of RAML is based on RAML v0.8. It is not a replacement for a complete and thorough introduction to RAML. This section intends to provide some initial ideas for the use of RAML. Detailed information is available on http://raml.org [13].

RAML is based on YAML [29]. YAML describes hierarchical data structures - similar to XML, but uses whitespace for structuring. Compared to XML, YAML is more lightweight and more readable. A YAML file consists of properties, which are realized as key-value pairs, objects or lists. Keys are strings and values can be primitive types or lists. Lists are presented in squared brackets [ ], e.g. `securedBy: [oauth_1_0, oauth_2_0 ]`. There can also be lists of properties, in this case a minus - is used in front of the property. Objects have child properties, which are indented by whitespace.

An API description in RAML contains the following main information items:

- Basic information and meta information about the API, such as name, title, location and user documentation. This information is captured in the root element.

- Resources including methods, schemas and parameters.

- Reusable elements including resource types, traits and security declarations.

Example

Let's get started by describing the Book API portfolio in RAML. It is the same API portfolio we have used in the previous section for the description in Swagger. This API portfolio contains two APIs, one collection API delivering a listing of all available books written in a given language, and a book API providing details for a specific book, which is identified by an ISBN. In the following we describe this API portfolio in RAML.

```
#%RAML 0.8
title: Book API
baseUri: https://domain.com/{version}
version: v1
mediaType: application/json
protocols: [https]
documentation:
  - title: Start page for the documentation of the API
    content: |
      The book API ...
resourceTypes:
  - collection:
      get:
        description: returning a list of elements,
                     which are part of the collection
      post:
        description: adding a new element to the
collection
traits:
  - languageSelection:
      queryParameters:
        lang:
          type: string
/books:
  type: collection
  get:
    is: [ languageSelection ]
    /{isbn}:
```

```
uriParameters:
  isbn:
    type: string
get:
  responses:
    200:
      body:
        application/json:
          schema: |
            { "$schema": "http://json-
                          schema.org/schema",
              "type": "object",
              "description": "A book",
              "properties": {
                 "title": { "type": "string" },
                 "author": { "type": "string" },
                 "price": { "type": "number" },
                 "isbn": { "type": "string" },
                 "language": { "type": "string" },
                 "description": { "type": "string"}
              },
              "required": [ "title",
                            "author",
                            "isbn" ]
            }
          example: |
            { "title": "Walden",
              "author": "Henry David Thoreau",
              "price": 8.90,
              "isbn": "123456789X",
              "language": "en",
              "description": "A reflection on
                              simple living in
                              nature"
            }
```

All language elements you can find in the above example are explained in the following subsections.

Root Element

As you can see from the example, RAML is a hierarchical language. Sub elements are indented relative to their parent element. The parent element of them all is the root element at the top of the RAML description. It is used to specify some basic information. It includes the following properties:

- `title:` The title is a human readable name of the API.

- `baseUri:` The baseUri points to a running instance of the API or of an API simulation. The version can be part of the baseUri and can be referenced as a URI template parameter.

- `version:` The version of the API.

- `mediaType:` The mediaType specified in the root element is the default media type for this API portfolio. It can be overwritten per method.

- `protocols:` The protocols in the root element are the default protocols. It can be overwritten per method.

- `schemas:` Schemas define data structures, typically in the form of JSON schemas or XML schemas. They can be specified inline or can be included from an external file.

- `documentation:` User documentation is provided in the form of a title and some descriptive text.

- `securitySchemes:` Predefined security packages.

- `traits:` Reusable parts for a method definition.

- `resourceTypes:` Reusable parts for a resource definition.

Resources

Resources are direct child elements of the root and are identified by their relative URI. The resource URI must begin with a slash (/). Resources can be nested, where nesting is expressed by indenting the relative URI.

Methods

For each resource it is defined, which HTTP methods may be executed. All basic HTTP methods are supported, such as GET, POST, PUT and DELETE. Multiple HTTP methods can be used for each URI.

```
#%RAML 0.8
title: Book API
/books:
  get:
    responses: !include get.raml
  post:
    responses: !include post.raml
```

Responses

For each HTTP method multiple responses can be specified. The responses are identified using HTTP response codes. Each response consists of a specification for header and body.

```
#%RAML 0.8
title: Book API
/books:
  get:
    responses:
      200:
        body: !include body.raml
        header: !include header.raml
```

```
400:
  description: Invalid Request
500:
  description: Internal Server Error
```

The body is specified by providing the content type, a schema definition and an additional example. Multiple representations of the same resource can be served on the same URI, same method and same response code. The representations are differentiated only by the content type.

```
#%RAML 0.8
title: Book API
/books:
  get:
    responses:
      200:
        body:
          application/json:
            schema: !include book.json
            example: |
              { "title": "Walden",
                "author": "Henry David Thoreau",
                "price": 8.90,
                "isbn": "123456789X",
                "description": "A reflection on simple
                                living in nature"
              }
```

Schema

The schema definition is expressed as JSON Schema [25]. The schema can be declared inline or it can be included from an external source.

```
#%RAML 0.8
title: Book API
/books/{isbn}:
  uriParameters:
    isbn:
      type: string
  get:
    responses:
      200:
        body:
          application/json:
            schema: |
              { "$schema": "http://json-
                            schema.org/schema",
                "type": "object",
                "description": "A book",
                "properties": {
                    "title":   { "type": "string" },
                    "author": { "type": "string" },
                    "price":   { "type": "number" },
                    "isbn":   { "type": "string" },
                    "description": { "type": "string" }
                },
                "required": ["title", "author", "isbn"]
              }
```

Parameters

In RAML, path parameters are declared as properties of the resource and all other types of parameters are declared as properties of the method. All named parameters have the following properties:

- `displayName`: A human readable name.

- `description`: Documentation of the parameter.

- `type:` Data type of the parameter. The data type can be `string`, `number`, `integer`, `data`, `boolean`, `file`.

- `enum:` For parameters of type string, enum allows to define a list of all valid string values.

- `pattern:` A regular expression (ECMA 262/Perl 5) that values must satisfy.

- `minLength:` Minimum number of characters in a string value.

- `maxLength:` Maximum number of characters in a string value.

- `minimum:` Minimum integer value.

- `maximum:` Maximum integer value.

- `example:` Example value for this parameter.

- `repeat:` Indicates how many times the parameter can occur.

- `required:` Indicates if the parameter must be present (true/false).

- `default:` default value for this parameter.

Path Parameters

Path parameters are called uriParameters in RAML. They are declared on two locations. The location of the value of the path parameter is marked by the parameter name in curly braces within the relative URI path.

To provide additional information about the parameters, it is also listed under the `uriParameters` element. This allows for the declaration of the parameter type and any of the other parameter properties listed above.

The books API can be called by

```
GET /books/123
```

```
#%RAML 0.8
title: Book API
/books/{isbn}
  uriParameters:
    isbn:
      type: string
```

Query Parameters

Query parameters can be declared for each HTTP method separately. The books API can be called by

```
GET /books?isbn=123
```

```
#%RAML 0.8
title: Book API
/books:
  get:
    queryParameters:
      isbn:
        type: string
```

Form Parameters

Form parameters can be declared for each HTTP method separately.

The books API can be called by

```
POST /books
```

The body contains for example `isbn=123`

```
#%RAML 0.8
title: Book API
/books:
  post:
    formParameters:
      isbn:
        type: string
```

Header Parameters

Header parameters can be declared for each HTTP method separately. The books API can be called by

```
GET /books
```

The HTTP header contains for example the entry `isbn: 123`.

```
#%RAML 0.8
title: Book API
/books:
  get:
    headers:
      isbn:
        type: string
```

Reusable Elements

The description of a consistent API portfolio can be quite repetitive. Repeatedly used elements should be factored out and thus become reusable elements. Reusable elements are declared once and referenced several times. In RAML, there are two categories of reusable elements. External reusable elements can be included from separate files and internal reusable elements can be referenced from the same RAML file.

External Elements: Inclusion of Files

RAML offers the a possibility to include the content of an external file. The referenced file is inlined by a pre-processor. Including an external file is a form of reuse.

External reusable elements can be the right hand side of any YAML declaration, i.e. anything right of the colon. In the following example, the property with name external retrieves its value from an included text file.

```
external: !include myTextFile.txt
```

Internal Elements: Definition of Resource Types and Traits

Resource types and traits are specified for providing reuse within the same RAML file. A resource type is a partial resource definition; resource types are thus applied on resource definitions. A trait is a partial method definition; traits are thus applied on methods.

Resource types and traits are defined in the root element of the RAML document. In the following section we show how the resource types and traits can be applied inside API specifications.

```
#%RAML 0.8
title: Book API
version: v1
resourceTypes:
  - collection:
      get:
        description: returning a list of elements,
                     which are part of the collection
      post:
        description: adding a new element to the
                     collection
        is: [ languageSelection ]
traits:
  - languageSelection:
      queryParameters:
        lang:
          type: string
```

As a side note: A trait can even be used for defining a resource type. This possibility is shown in the above example. The trait languageSelection is used within the definition of the resource type collection.

Internal Elements: Usage of Resource Types and Traits

Resource types are applied by the keyword type: as a direct child of the resource. Traits are applied on method level or on resource level by the keyword is: followed by a list of the applied traits in squared brackets [ ]. If the trait is applied on resource level, it applies to all methods of this resource.

```
#%RAML 0.8
title: Book API
/books:
  type: collection
  get:
    is: [ languageSelection ]
```

144

Security

RAML language constructs for security describe how the API is protected. This is usually a two-step approach. First, one or several `securitySchemes` are configured. Then these securitySchemes are bound to an API, to a resource or to a specific HTTP method of a resource via the keyword `securedBy`. By using this two-step approach, it is easy to achieve a consistent application of the same securitySchemes on several resources and APIs.

A securityScheme is basically a configuration, which specifies the type of the security mechanism (OAuth 1.0, OAuth 2.0, Basic, Digest, or a wildcard for another mechanism), the available OAuth grant types, available OAuth scopes, parameters, headers, responses and URIs of the different OAuth endpoints. The securitySchemes need to be declared as part of the root element. Security schemes, e.g. for OAuth, can be defined inline or -- more often -- in separate files.

```
#%RAML 0.8
title: Book API
securitySchemes:
    - oauth_2_0:
        description: |
            OAuth 2.0 security mechanism.
        type: OAuth 2.0
        describedBy:
            headers:
                Authorization:
                    description: |
                        Send the OAuth 2 access token as
                        Bearer token in the
                        Authorization Header
                    type: string
            responses:
                400:
                    description: |
                        Invalid request.
                401:
                    description: |
```

```
                    Bad or expired token.
          403:
              description: |
                Bad OAuth request.
      settings:
        authorizationUri:
          https://domain.com/oauth2/auth
        accessTokenUri:
          https://domain.com/oauth2/token
        authorizationGrants: [ code, token ]
        scopes: [administrator, user]
```

In a second step, the defined securitySchemes can be bound to APIs, resources or methods. There are two ways to do this: either as default security, or as security for a specific API, resource or method.

- Default security is applied to all resources of the API. This can be achieved by applying the keyword `securedBy` on the root element.

- The default can be overwritten by specifying the `securedBy` keyword on the respective API, resource or method.

When applying securitySchemes with the `securedBy` keyword, a list of allowed securitySchemes can be specified. If this list contains more than one element, the listed securitySchemes are alternatives.

```
#%RAML 0.8
title: API
version: v3
baseUri: https://domain.com
securitySchemes:
- oauth_2_0: !include oauth_2_0.raml
securedBy: [ oauth_2_0 ]
/admin:
  get:
    securedBy: [ oauth_2_0: { scopes: [ administrator
], authorizationGrants: [code] } ]
```

For each securityScheme, additional parameters can be specified, such as the OAuth scopes and OAuth grant types, which are required for this particular element. The scopes and grant types, which are listed under securedBy should be a subset of the available scopes and grant types that were declared in the securitySchemes.

Summary

API description languages are very powerful tools for API architecture. Proficiency in one of the main API description languages is essential for designing an API portfolio and its API proxies efficiently. In the following chapter we show how to make the best possible use of API descriptions by consistently applying them throughout the API development process.

API Methodology

An API methodology is supposed to provide an answer to the question: How should I design and develop my APIs?

Many methodologies for proper API design and development have been proposed and are still the subject of passionate debates. The design and development of APIs, however, is a topic that is too complex to deliver a step-by-step "How To" guide. Instead, think of this methodology as a guideline, which provides some goalposts along the way, that were constructed based on past failures, experiences and learnings.

There is no right or wrong methodology, but there is a methodology that fits into a specific company culture better than others. This is why we present a API design and development methodology consisting of some coarse granular phases that you can pick and choose from to ensure that the methodology you use for your company actually fits your company culture. This is one of the best ways to make sure that the API methodology is actually applied by the team.

Foundations

In the proposed API methodology we use best practices for design, such as consumer-oriented design, contract first design, iterative design and simulation-based design. In the following we introduce these best practices and show why and how they apply to API design.

Consumer-oriented Design Approach

There are two basic methodological approaches. They are known under the names inside-out approach and outside-in approach, depending on the starting point and the direction of the design process. We propose the outside-in approach because it is consumer-oriented. We mention the inside-out approach as well to contrast and clarify the differences.

Inside-out Approach

The starting point for the inside-out approach is an analysis of what already exists inside the organization of the API provider. For API providers, the backend systems already exist inside the organization and are used as a basis for defining the API.

The design of an API developed with the inside-out approach will closely resemble the structure of the backend system. Using this approach, an API could be built just by forwarding calls to backends, optionally some data format transformations and some protocol transformations.

This approach is quite simple from the perspective of the API provider, since the functional scope of the API is confined by one backend system. The complexities of aggregating information from multiple backend systems are reduced. For the API provider this approach might seem to be the natural choice.

Even though building the API may be simple from the perspective of the API provider, it might be quite complex to use the API for the API consumers, since they are confronted with the complex data structures of the backends. Such an API is not likely to be consumer friendly.

Outside-in Approach

In a way, the outside-in approach is the opposite to the inside-out approach. The starting point for the outside-in approach is an analysis of what is needed by the consumers. The consumers are outside the organization of the API provider, thus the API provider needs to start the design process outside his organization and gradually work his way back in. Only in the last step of this approach, the API provider may make considerations about what is inside the organization: the data formats, and the connections to existing backends.

This approach certainly means more work on the side of the API provider, but there is a larger chance that a consumer-friendly API is produced.

Why is a consumer friendly API important? A measure for the success of an API initiative is the wide-spread use of the API: the API should be used by as many consumers as possible. To maximize the uptake of APIs with potential consumers, to maximize the active usage of the API and to maximize the integration in third party apps, the API needs to be as simple as possible from the perspective of the consumer.

The basic idea of the outside-in approach is to focus on the consumers. One needs to identify the target consumers first and then get to know their needs. This allows for designing an optimal experience for the interaction between the consumer and the API. For the API provider it is thus important to ask: What would the consumer want to achieve by using the API? How can I make it easy for the consumer to find the API? How can I help the consumer to build apps with my API and make it convenient for the consumer to use the API?

Contract First Design Approach

In contract first design, the central artifact is an explicit contract between API provider and API consumer. Such a contract is either dictated by the provider or better, it is specified by provider and consumer together.

In this contract, the API provider guarantees certain exactly specified APIs to the consumer. Based on this contract, the consumer can already start implementing a solution in parallel with API development.

Agile Design Approach

Agility is based on the premise that you can start without having a full set of specs. You can always adapt and change the specs later, as you go and as you have learned more. Through multiple iterations, architectural design can converge to the right solution. If the iterations are performed based on the architectural blueprint and not based on a full implementation, architecture improves the overall efficiency of development.

However, is the agile approach 100% compatible with the the requirements for APIs?

- Before publishing the API, the API can be changed and the agile approach can be used. Change is easy and possible at any time.

- After publishing the API, changes become difficult. If a published API changes, clients could get broken. New versions need to be created for each API change that is not backward compatible. The interface specs are fully defined and thus the prerequisites for agility are no longer given.

An agile approach should only be applied, until the API is published.

Simulation-based Design

Basically every software system has dependencies to other software, such as other software components, libraries and frameworks. Due to these dependencies, some components cannot be developed until the development of their dependencies has been completed. This enforces sequential development, limits the possibilities for parallel development and requires a longer development time. The result is a long time-to market for the complete software system.

Simulations offer a solution: they make it possible to break up the dependencies between software components and allow for integration and development of software components, even though their dependencies have not been developed, yet. Dependencies are replaced by simulations.

In API design there are two use cases for simulations:

- The simulation of backend systems allows for developing APIs without fully implemented backend systems.

- The simulation of APIs allows for developing apps (or other API solutions) without fully implemented APIs.

Simulation of Backends

Since APIs depend on the backend systems and their behavior, the implementation of an API can only start after the backend has become available. If the backend has not been finalized yet, the development of the API is blocked and the API cannot be built.

Simulations of backend systems can be used to support the development of APIs. Backend simulations break the dependencies from APIs to backends. If the real backend is not available yet, a simulation of the backend can be used in its place. Since the behavior of the simulation is the same as the behavior of the real backend, the implementation of the API with a simulated backend can proceed independently of the availability of the implementation of the backend.

Simulation of the API

The development of an API solution, such as a mobile app, depends on the availability of the included APIs. If the APIs are not available, the development of the mobile app is blocked.

Simulations of APIs can support the development of mobile apps, which depend on the APIs. Even though the API has not been implemented yet, the mobile app can be built and the API can be integrated. The development of the API and the development of the mobile app can take place in parallel. The simulation speeds up the development time of the overall API solution, and allows for short time to market.

Ideally, the API description is detailed enough to serve as a specification for the simulation.

Requirements for an API Methodology

An API solution has a certain complexity. Complexity does not simply go away -- it has to be handled somewhere, by someone. Thus, the complexity of the API solution can either be dealt with in the client or in the API.

If the complexity is dealt with in the client, the task of the API provider is simple and the task of the API consumer is difficult. This is usually the result of the inside-out approach and leads to sub-optimal APIs that make the life of the API consumer unnecessarily hard.

If the complexity is dealt with in the API, the task of the API provider is difficult. However, the task of the API consumer is simple. This is usually the result of the outside-in approach. An outside-in approach has a higher chance of producing APIs that consumers love and despite the difficulties for the API provider, it is the recommended approach.

Since building consumer-oriented APIs with the outside-in approach is rather difficult for the API provider, as much methodological support as possible should be given to the API provider. This includes contract-first design, agile design and simulation-based design.

Applying the contract-first ideas to API design, allows for a clear separation of the responsibility between API and client.

Applying an agile approach can help to navigate in situations with unclear or vague requirements, but should only be applied until the API is published.

Applying ideas of the simulation approach allows for breaking up the dependencies during development. It allows for an independent development of client and API, despite the dependencies between them.

Methodology

This methodology is an outside-in approach and also incorporates ideas of contract-first design, the agile approach and simulation-based development. In this methodology, the contract is expressed in the form of an API description. In each step of the methodology, an API description is either created, refined or used -- the API description is the red thread connecting all the steps of the methodology.

Overview

Let's start with an overview of the phases in this API methodology. Each phase of this methodology consists of a creative part and a verification part. During the creative part an artifact is crafted, during the verification part early feedback on the artifact is collected. In each phase along the design and development journey, feedback from the consumers is elicited. It is important to collect the feedback as early as possible, when changes to the API are still possible, relatively simple and can be implemented with low effort at a relatively low cost.

This methodology is meant to be used iteratively. There are small iterations, which are triggered by the verification part of the same phase. There are also big iterations, which are triggered by one of the later verification phases and require going back to the creative part of an earlier phase. Keep in mind, that in an iterative and agile approach, not all information and requirements about the constructed artifact are present in the beginning, but new and more detailed information and insights are gathered in each iteration.

The API methodology consists of the following phases:

1. Domain analysis

2. Architectural design

3. Prototyping

4. Building API software for production

5. Publishing the API

Phase 1: Domain Analysis

The goal of the first phase is to analyze the "problem domain", identify resources and sketch a simple API description for each resource. This API description can be verified by simulation and integration into a demo app.

The first step of a domain analysis phase is gaining some clarity on the needs of the consumer and possible usage scenarios. Sketching usage scenarios is a creative act.

Start by asking yourself:

- Who are the consumers of the API?

- What is the purpose of the API?

- Which API solutions do the consumers plan to build with the API?

- Which other API solutions would be possible with the API?

Even though the development of new APIs is usually triggered by a concrete project, the goal should be the development of a generic API. Thus, not only the usage scenario at hand should be sketched and not only the obvious usage scenario. Ideally, a broad set of usage scenarios for the API should be sketched. Sketching can be either in some form of graphics or in the form of text.

The next step is to build a resource taxonomy for the given usage scenarios. Think from a consumer's perspective about the usage scenario, try not to have the tinted view of some existing backend structure or existing database tables, since those snap you back to the internal viewpoint.

Take on the API consumers' point of view. How would an API look like that they want to use? What apps would they want to build? What data objects would they want to use in their apps?

To create a taxonomy, write down the usage scenario, then select the nouns in the text. Shortlist the nouns that would make sense as resources, i.e. nouns that describe data objects, which the operations create, read, update or delete can be performed on. As part of the taxonomy creation, one needs to analyze the relationships between the resources:

- A dependent resource cannot exist without the other.

- An independent resource on the other hand can exist without any other resource.

- Associative resources exist independently but still have some kind of relation., e.g. they may be connected by reference.

The next step is to think about the states of the resources and possible transitions between the resource states.

The resources in the taxonomy have states and during the execution of the app, the resources may change their states and transition into new states. Express the states and transitions in a state diagram.

Which insights can we gather from the state diagram? The states provide an indicator for the resources that are needed. The transitions in the diagram provide an indicator for the HTTP methods that need to be supported.

With the information collected during domain analysis, a first API description can be built. Admittedly, this first model is rather a sketch than an architecture, but it still allows defining the API resources, their vocabulary, and which operations will manipulate those resources.

Verification of Phase 1: Simulation & Demo App

A good simulation allows us to answer some questions about a planned system without having to spend all the effort of building that system. At this stage, the simulation can help to define the purpose of the API: Does it make sense to build an API with the given functionality for the usage scenarios at hand? Does the sketched API help me build the solution? Are the requirements of the API properly captured in the API description?

To answer these questions, a first, low-fidelity API prototype should be built. Such an early prototype should only be built, when the effort for creating the prototype is minimal. This is why the API prototype should not be implemented manually, but it should be constructed automatically by generating a simulation based on the API description. Frameworks for API description languages offer such capabilities for generating simulations.

The simulation provides a verification of the stand-alone API. More effective would be a verification of the API in the context of a solution: to verify that the API is relevant and usable, the integrated API needs to be verified in the context of an API solution or app. This is not necessarily an app with real requirements. A simple demo app for an artificial problem is sufficient for this phase. The simplest demo app would be a little bit more than a curl call. The demo app provides a showcase for the API and can be reused in later stages.

Phase 2: Architectural Design

During the architectural design phase, the API description created in phase 1, is refined. First of all, an appropriate architectural style should be chosen, such as REST, RPC or HATEOAS. In a second step, architectural design should make decisions about:

- Protocols
- Endpoints
- URI design
- Security
- Performance and availability
- Quotas and traffic shaping

These design decisions should be documented by refining and updating the API description. The API description thus becomes an evolving, single source of truth about the current state of the system.

Once the bigger-picture, architectural design decisions are nailed, detailed design decisions can be handled. For the REST architectural style, these design decisions include:

- Resources
- Representations

162

- Content types

- Parameters

- HTTP methods

- HTTP status codes

- Consistent naming

As before, the detailed design decisions are documented by refining the API description.

In addition to the above design decisions, it should be avoided to reinvent the wheel for common APIs. Instead, existing API templates (such as those found on http://apicommons.org) should be used. APIs should also be designed as a part of the API portfolio. Design decisions should be consistent across all APIs of the portfolio.

Verification of Phase 2: Simulation & Demo App

A simulation should be used at this point to quickly verify the effects of the architectural and detailed design decisions. The following questions might help to verify the design: Is the API still easy to use? Is it still a small, agile and usable API or did we create a monster API? Does this API help us to realize our usage scenarios? Does the API follow the architectural style selected?

Ideally, the changes that are necessary to the API description at this stage are minimal. The API description should become stable.

As part of the verification, the API description can be handed over to pilot consumers, so they can base the design of their API solution, such as their mobile app, on our design. The demo app created in the previous phase can be reused for integration testing of the simulated API.

Phase 3: Prototyping

> "Plan to throw one away; you will anyhow. "
> -- Frederick P. Brooks

Prototyping is a preparation phase for the productive implementation. One goal of prototyping is to learn as many practical insights as possible while spending as little effort as possible. This can be achieved by quickly creating a simple prototype implementation, that you plan to throw away. Not every aspect of the API should be implemented in this phase, only the critical aspects of the API should be assessed.

The prototype implementation will be tested by pilot consumers. There are thus two goals for proper prototyping: practical insights into critical implementation issues and a low effort for the creation of the prototype.

The first goal is to gain practical insights through the prototyping effort. To gain some learning with practical relevance, the API prototype needs to be as realistic as possible. While simulations can be considered to be low-fidelity prototypes, this phase creates high-fidelity prototypes that are more realistic, more relevant and closer to the actual implementation. The API prototype should conform to the API description and use real data from real backends.

At the same time, there is the second goal, which requires the prototype to be built as quickly as possible and with as little effort and budget as possible. To achieve the necessary speed, the implementation does not have to be pretty, does not have to be optimized and may contain engineering shortcuts.

To fulfill both goals, code generation can be used. Code generation for API proxies is offered for all API description languages. Properly generated code conforms to the API description. However, the generated code has "holes", only the interface of the API can be generated. The generated code is merely a skeleton. It provides some structure and the correct interface, but the "meat", the implementation, has to be added manually around the skeleton. The missing code can be added with relatively low effort, since the skeleton already provides a structure.

So which implementation tasks need to be done during this phase? This needs to be decided on a case-by-case basis. If the real backends are available, they may be integrated, otherwise a simulation of the backend is used. Requests and responses of the backends need to be transformed, input and output need to be validated and security needs to be implemented and configured, just to name a few. Some implementation details can be left out at this stage, such as traffic shaping or performance optimizations.

An API prototype is always an imperfect and incomplete implementation of the API. Actually, the prototype implementation has to be incomplete, otherwise too much time has been scheduled for realizing the prototype. To maximize the learnings from prototyping, one should focus on implementing the aspects, which are most critical. For one API, the backend connection may be on the critical path, for another API, it may be a complex input validation algorithm. Focus on these critical issues and use shortcuts for the other issues to get to a testable prototype quickly. If the backend connection is not on the critical path, the prototype API does need to be connected to the real backend and a simulation of the backend is sufficient at this stage.

For simple APIs without any critical issues or the need to learn anything before implementation, one might be able to hop over the prototyping phase and go directly to the implementation phase.

165

Validation of Phase 3: Acceptance Tests with Pilot Consumers

API prototypes are usually built to answer the question "What are the major hurdles for building this API?" Besides exploring the feasibility, the prototype can be used for acceptance tests by pilot consumers. Let' s see what this means.

In general, an acceptance test is a black-box testing method, where users test if the specifications and requirements of a system are met. Acceptance tests are used to verify the completeness of a system. In our case, API consumers test the API prototype. Ideally, they use the API, when designing or building their app. In an acceptance test of the API, the consumers answer the question "Does this API provide some value for my app?"

Pilot consumers need to be API consumers, who are willing to work with unfinished APIs with changing interfaces, broken clients, frequent updates, unavailability and low performance of the API. In short: a pilot customer must be able to bear some pain. This is why pilot consumers are typically recruited from inside the organization of the API provider, for example from a department of the API provider. In some environments, pilot consumers are also called beta testers. Ideally, the pilot consumer writes an app that solves a real problem, sometimes a pilot consumer may just write a demo app for testing the API.

Why would an API provider voluntarily become an pilot consumer? The advantage for pilot consumers is early access to innovative APIs, allowing for short time-to-market of the consumer's app. This is an advantage that should not be underestimated in an ecosystem, where time-to-market has high impact on the market share.

Besides the validation by pilot consumers, the API prototype should also be checked for conformance with the API descriptions. To some extent, conformance between implementation and API description is already ensured by code generation. However, generated code may have been changed and manually added code may still need to be checked. Such a test should include JSON well-formedness checks and JSON schema validation of the results. Both of these tests can be generated from the API description. Additional tests might need to be added manually.

Phase 4: Implementation for Production

The implementation for production has similar constraints as the prototype implementation described in the previous section. The implementation needs to conform to the API description and needs to be delivered as quickly as possible. In addition, the API is fully integrated into the API portfolio. The goal of properly engineering software systems, is to ensure not only the correct functional but also the correct non-functional aspects. Some of the most important non-functional aspects of APIs are security, performance, and availability.

When an API has reached this phase of the methodology, the API description has been properly designed, has gone through several feedback loops has been verified from several perspectives. The API description should thus be stable. Just as in the previous phase, the stable and verified API description is used as a blueprint for automatically generating an API implementation skeleton. Automatic code generation ensures that the implementation is consistent with the API description, and thus is consistent with all the design decisions the description embodies.

However, the generated code is merely a code skeleton. The behavior of the API needs to be implemented manually, by filling in the gaps of the code skeleton. In the previous phase, the feasibility of the implementation has been shown, critical aspects of the implementation have already been tested and many insights have been gained. These insights are now applied during the implementation phase.

The focus of the implementation in this phase is thus, the proper engineering of the API. Proper software engineering practices need to be used. For example, common patterns should be identified, factored out into libraries, so they can be reused across the API portfolio.

Production systems also need to exhibit appropriate non-functional properties. The security of the API needs to be ensured. This can be achieved by choosing and enforcing adequate security mechanisms. The availability and performance of the API need to be ensured. These properties can be ensured by applying rate limitation and caching.

Verification of Phase 4: Acceptance Tests with Pilot Consumers

The set of pilot consumers typically grows as the API matures. The first group of pilot consumers used in the prototyping stage may consist of internal consumers of the API provider. As the API matures, the set of pilot consumers may evolve into a number of hand-picked API consumers.

Phase 5: Publish

Publishing an API does not require a lot of work, but it is a big milestone for the API.

From an organizational perspective, the responsibility of the API is transferred from the development unit to the operations unit. But most importantly, the API and its documentation become publicly available, API consumers will start building API clients and start using the API.

Publishing the API also means freezing its interface specification. After publishing, there is no agility in the development process any longer. Changes on published APIs require a traditional change management process.

For each published API, the API provider has an implicit contract with all its API consumers, which states the interface of the API. This is why once an API gets published, its interface can never change and the API needs to be maintained for a long time. Publishing an API implies a long-term commitment for maintaining it.

Publishing an API requires an appropriate documentation for consumers.

It almost goes without saying that the documentation needs to be consistent with the implementation. Sometimes, however, the problem is that the implementation gets changed during maintenance or redesign, but the documentation is not updated. This can be avoided by generating both the implementation skeleton and the documentation from the same single source of truth, from the API description.

Verification of Phase 5: Study Metrics, Reports and Logs

It is the expectation for a published API that an increasing number of consumers successfully use the API. To be able to find out if and how this expectation is actually fulfilled by the API, usage of the API has to be monitored, measured and analyzed.

169

Some of the metrics, which might be interesting in this context are: the total number of API calls per time frame, the number of API calls per consumer, and how many API calls resulted in an error vs in success. Not only quantitative analysis is relevant, but also some qualitative analysis.

Qualitative analysis includes for example understanding and categorizing the solutions, which the API consumers build with the API. An API provider would like to discover if API consumers use the API as intended or if they use the API in new ways that were never imagined by the API provider at the outset. Which of the usage scenarios were correctly predicted and which new usage scenarios evolved? This can also be a trigger point to find out if a new version of the API is needed and to determine if it needs to be redesigned.

For a quantitative analysis, the first step is to determine the usage of the API. The second step is to determine how successful the API is in contributing to the API solution. The third step is to draw conclusions, discover patterns in the usage, compare all the APIs in the portfolio. A relevant metric is the number successful API calls, especially if compared to the number of unsuccessful API calls. Do some API consumers have trouble getting the API to work as intended? Are there lots of error messages? Analyses according to this metric could be a trigger for updating the API documentation or redesigning the API.

Metrics are not only interesting to the API provider, but also to the API consumers. They are interested in API analytics, dashboards, reports and monitoring. The service availability metrics such as status reports, up-time and response time should not only be available to the API provider, but also to the consumers.

The API provider needs to continuously evaluate if the business objectives are met and if the business objectives are still up to date. Metrics allow for calculating business value and the ROI for the API provider. Metrics allow for understanding the consumers and marketing to them better. Based on the feedback gained and the insights obtained from analytics, the provider can improve the API.

Metrics based on consumer behavior are the real feedback for the success of the API. They allow for measuring if the adoption is as expected and if the revenue is as expected.

Even for successful APIs, the business or market might change and require a review if the API is still adequate for the market as it is today. API needs to be easy to adjust to react to changing market needs, business needs or problems with the API in a quick and agile manner.

Maintenance

The simple rule for API evolution is, that the externally observable behavior of an API (from the perspective of the clients) cannot be changed, once the API has been published. Already a small change to the API might break some of the clients consuming the API. It is impossible to update all the consumers or at least unrealistic, since they are under control of different owners. Thus, longevity and stability are important aspects of published APIs.

The restriction imposed by this rule might sound severe and even counter-intuitive, since APIs are often developed using an agile development approach. Agile approaches are based on feedback loops and the idea of many incremental changes of the software. The agile development methodology still applies to new or unpublished APIs.

Before the publication of the API, any change can be implemented in an agile manner. As soon as the API is published, however, the game changes. When APIs are published, they become available for consumers and it has to be assumed that the consumers build apps relying on the APIs. Published APIs cannot be changed in an agile manner. At least, APIs need to stay backward (and forward) compatible, so that old clients do not break and new clients can use the new and improved features.

Discussion

Hand-over Points

In this methodology, the contract is expressed in the form of an API description. In each phase of the methodology, an API description is either created, refined or used -- the API description is the red thread connecting all the steps of the methodology.

When can the API description be handed over to pilot consumers? Pilot consumers need to be patient and they need to be aware of the fact that their clients might break, since the API description might still change. The earliest point in time at which a hand-over of the API description makes sense, is after the architectural and detailed design phase has been finished, the API description has been created and has been simulated successfully.

When is the API description finished? The API description is only really finished, when the API has been published, in the final phase of the methodology. After publishing the API, the API description is frozen and cannot be changed without breaking potential clients.

Pre-Work vs. Actual Work

When you look at the proposed methodology, you can see that a lot of "pre-work" is done, before the actual implementation for production starts. Is this a waste of time?

No, this pre-work is required so the API is stable and does not need to be changed changed shortly after publication. Once an API is published, an implicit (and sometimes even explicit) contract between API provider and API consumer is set up. In this contract, the API provider agrees to support the API for some time into the future, and will not make any changes that might break the client.

For the consumers this contract means that they can rely on the API to be around for a while and thus dare to build solutions, which rely on this API.

For the API provider, however, this contract is also constraining. The contract binds the API provider to support the API. Changes are not possible on the published API. If the API provider notices too late (i.e. after publishing) that the API should actually look and behave differently, the existing API cannot just be updated, since this would break the existing clients.

Both parties are better off, when investing into the "pre-work" for design and verification, before beginning the "actual work" of implementation.

Summary

Many methodologies for proper API design and development have been proposed and these methodologies are subject of passionate debates. However, there is no wrong or right methodology, but there is a methodology that fits into a specific company culture better than others.

This is why we propose that you pick and choose the phases or steps from this design and development methodology to ensure that it really fits your culture. This is one of the best ways to make sure that the API methodology is actually adopted and lived by the team.

176

Conclusion

In all technical discussions about APIs it should not be forgotten, that none of these topics is as important as satisfied API consumers. If API consumers are satisfied with the API and use it, it does not matter if your REST design is compatible with every aspect of Roy Fieldings thesis.

When building APIs, you need to focus on the API consumer. An API needs to be simple from the API consumer's perspective. How to build APIs that target the consumer? Sometimes you don't know from the beginning who the consumers are, or what they want. Sometimes you might only gradually find out, what the needs of API consumers are.

What does this mean for the API provider that needs to build APIs? An API provider might need to bend over backwards to build APIs that are simple for the consumers. This also means that API implementation might become a bit more complex.

To deal with this complexity, API providers need some structure, tools and methods. This book provides a structure for building consumer-focused APIs. We call this structure API architecture; it consists of the solution architecture, platform architecture, portfolio architecture, proxy architecture.

Some practical guidelines

Learn about the **solution architecture** of your consumers. Become clear on who your API consumers are, which solutions they want to build and what they expect from your API.

Choose a **platform architecture** that simplifies your work as API provider as much as possible and serves as a solid as a foundation for your APIs. The platform should not only support API development, but also API operation and API consumer engagement.

Do not merely design isolated API proxies. Instead, design each API proxy as a part of the **API portfolio architecture**. Design this portfolio to be consistent, reusable, findable and ready for evolution.

Use an API description language for specifying the **API proxy architecture** of each API in the portfolio. Use best practices, architectural patterns and styles for each API proxy.

Build your **design and development methodology** around your activities with the API description language. Use the API description language as the red thread connecting all your activities for the design and development of the API.

178

180

Backmatter

Feedback

If you have enjoyed this book and got some value from it, it would be great if you could share with others what you liked about the book on the Amazon review page.

If you feel something was missing or you are not satisfied with your purchase, please contact me at matt@api-university.com. I read this email personally and am very interested in your feedback.

About the Author

Matthias uses his background in software engineering to bring innovative software solutions to the market. Matthias has provided expertise to international and national companies on software architecture, software development processes and software integration. At some point he got a PhD.

As an expert in API management and mobile technologies, Matthias enjoys developing innovative products side-by-side with the clients and loves sharing his knowledge in the classroom, at workshops and in his books. Matthias is an instructor at the API-University, publishes a blog on APIs, is author of several books on APIs and regularly speaks at technology conferences.

Other Products by the Author

The API-University Series is a modular series of books on API-related topics. Each book focuses on a particular API topic, so you can select the topics within APIs, which are relevant for you.

OAuth 2.0: API Security Book

This book offers an introduction to API Security with OAuth 2.0. In less than 80 pages you will gain an overview of the capabilities of OAuth. You will learn the core concepts of OAuth. You will get to know all 4 OAuth Flows that are used in cloud solutions and mobile apps. If you have tried to read the official OAuth specification, you may get the impression that OAuth is complicated.

This book explains OAuth in simple terms. The different OAuth Flows are visualized graphically using sequence diagrams. The diagrams allow you to see the big picture of the various OAuth interactions. This high-level overview is complemented with a rich set of example requests and responses and an explanation of the technical details.

In the book the challenges and benefits of OAuth are presented, followed by an explanation of the technical concepts of OAuth. The technical concepts include the actors, endpoints, tokens and the four OAuth flows. Each flow is described in detail, including the use cases for each flow.

Available as paperback book and as kindle ebook:
http://api-university.com/books/oauth-2-0-book

API Design Book

Looking for best practices on building RESTful APIs? This book is for you!

This book is packed with best practices on technical aspects of RESTful API Design, including the correct use of resources, URIs, representations, content types, data formats, parameters, HTTP status codes and HTTP methods. It also includes best practices for evolution and versioning, security, performance and availability issues.

API description languages (RAML and Swagger) are introduced as a way to document your API design decisions.

An API development methodology is proposed to provide some guidance towards efficient API development.

Available as paperback book and as kindle ebook:
http://api-university.com/books/api-design

OAuth 2.0 Online Course

This course offers an introduction to API Security with OAuth 2.0. In 3 hours you will gain an overview of the capabilities of OAuth. You will learn the core concepts of OAuth. You will get to know all 4 OAuth flows that are used in cloud solutions and mobile apps.

Online Course:
http://api-university.com/courses/oauth-2-0-course/

References

1. IETF, URI Template, IETF RFC 6570, https://tools.ietf.org/html/rfc6570

2. IETF, Uniform Resource Identifier (URI): Generic Syntax, IETF RFC 3986, https://tools.ietf.org/html/rfc3986

3. IETF, HTTP Authentication: Basic and Digest Access Authentication, IETF RFC 2617, https://www.ietf.org/html/rfc2617

4. IETF, The OAuth 2.0 Authorization Framework, IETF RFC 6749, https://tools.ietf.org/html/rfc6749

5. Matthias Biehl, OAuth 2.0 - Getting Started in Web-API Security, 2015, ISBN-13: 978-1507800911

6. OpenID Connect 1.0, http://openid.net/specs/openid-connect-core-1_0.html

7. IETF, Hypertext Transfer Protocol -- HTTP/1.1, IETF RFC 2616, https://www.ietf.org/html/rfc2616

8. Roy Thomas Fielding's PhD dissertation "Architectural Styles and the Design of Network-based Software Architectures", http://www.ics.uci.edu/~fielding/pubs/dissertation/top.htm

9. IETF, UUID, IETF RFC 4122, https://tools.ietf.org/html/rfc4122

10. IETF, Timestamp, IETF RFC 3339, https://www.ietf.org/html/rfc3339

11. ECMA, ECMAScript/JavaScript, http://www.ecma-international.org/publications/files/ECMA-ST/Ecma-262.pdf

12. Swagger Language Specification, 2015, https://github.com/swagger-api/swagger-spec/blob/master/versions/2.0.md

13. RAML Language Specification, 2015, http://raml.org/spec

14. Mashery IO Docs, 2015, http://www.mashery.com/product/io-docs

15. API Blueprint, 2015, https://github.com/apiaryio/api-blueprint/blob/master/API%20Blueprint%20Specification.md

16. W3C, WSDL Web Services Description Language version 1.1, 2001, http://www.w3.org/TR/wsdl

17. W3C, WADL Web Application Description Language version 1.0, 2009, http://www.w3.org/Submission/wadl

18. Martin Fowler, Public versus Published Interfaces, 2002, http://martinfowler.com/ieeeSoftware/published.pdf

19. JSON RPC version 2, 2010, http://www.jsonrpc.org/specification

20. XML RPC version 2, 2013, http://www.jsonrpc.org/specification

21. W3C, SOAP version 1.2, 2007, http://www.w3.org/TR/soap12

22. IETF, WebSockets RFC 6455, 2011,
https://tools.ietf.org/html/rfc6455

23. IANA, Media Types Registry,
http://www.iana.org/assignments/media-types

24. Stefan Gössner, JSONPath, 2015,
http://goessner.net/articles/JsonPath

25. JSON Schema, http://json-schema.org

26. W3C, Extensible Markup Language (XML) 1.0, 2008,
http://www.w3.org/TR/xml

27. W3C, XPath 3.0, 2014, http://www.w3.org/TR/xpath-30

28. W3C, XML Schema, 2004,
http://www.w3.org/TR/xmlschema-1

29. YAML, 2009, http://www.yaml.org/spec

30. Matthias Biehl, API Design, API University, 2015

Image Sources

Thanks to Roberto Taddeo for providing permission to use his photography as cover picture.

Icons made by Freepik from www.flaticon.com are licensed under creative commons.

Printed in Great Britain
by Amazon.co.uk, Ltd.,
Marston Gate.